German Anti-Tank (Panzerjäger) Troops in World War II

Wolfgang Fleischer & Richard Eiermann

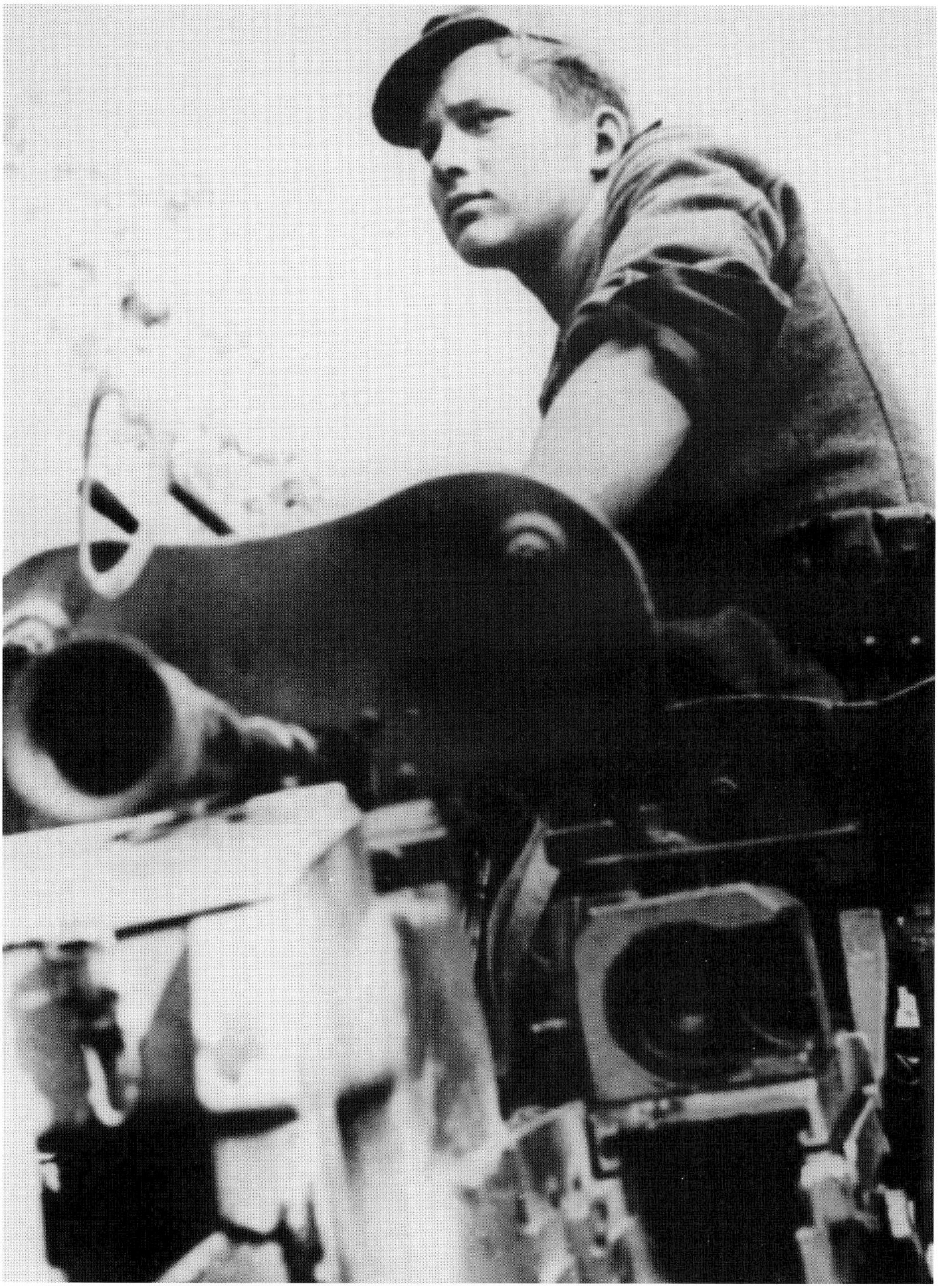

Antitank gunner with 2.8 cm Heavy Panzerbüchse 41. In the foreword of H.Dv. 470/6, Principles of Training of Antitank Units, the requirements for the soldier are formulated: "The battle against armored war vehicles . . . demands of every single man of the antitank bands tense watchfulness and lightning-fast actions."

German Anti-Tank (Panzerjäger) Troops in World War II

Wolfgang Fleischer
& Richard Eiermann

Schiffer Military History
Atglen, PA

Photo Credits

Federal Archives, Koblenz (48), Caye\ (2), Eiermann (35), Elser (4), Fabry (1), Faustka (3), Feist (1), Fleischer (125), Hoppe (23), MHM Dresden (1), Thiede (6), Schwetzingen City Archives (3), Wetzig (22).

Thanks

The authors would like to thank Ms. Wetzig of Dresden and Messrs. Elser (Oldenburg), Faustka (Vienna) and Hoppe (Berlin) for their support. Special thanks to Dr. Stang of Potsdam.

Translated from the German by Ed Force
Book design by Joseph M. Riggio Jr.

Library of Congress Catalog Number: 2004109057

This book was originally published under the title, *Panzerfahrzeuge und Panzereinheiten der Ordnungspolizei 1936-1945* by Podzun-Pallas.

Printed in China.
ISBN: 0-7643-2096-3

Published by Schiffer Publishing Ltd.
4880 Lower Valley Road
Atglen, PA 19310
Phone: (610) 593-1777
FAX: (610) 593-2002
E-mail: info@schifferbooks.com.
Visit our web site at: www.schifferbooks.com
Please write for a free catalog.
This book may be purchased from the publisher.
Please include $3.95 postage.
Try your bookstore first.
In Europe, Schiffer books are distributed by:
Bushwood Books
6 Marksbury Ave.
Kew Gardens
Surrey TW9 4JF
England
Phone: 44 (0)208 392-8585
FAX: 44 (0)208 392-9876
E-mail: info@bushwoodbooks.co.uk.
Free postage in the UK. Europe: air mail at cost.
Try your bookstore first.

CONTENTS

Contemporary drawing of tank destroyers on a postcard of the Tank Destroyer Replacement and Training Unit 33, Landau in the Palatinate.

FOREWORD

The massive use of armored combat vehicles (tanks) on the battlefields of World War I by the British and French armies was still burdened with numerous unsolved tactical and technical problems, but had granted this new weapon a firm place in the fighting forces. This was seen in postwar development, which was characterized by a great number of revised and new designs and an intense theoretical discussion of tanks and their uses. Some countries, including France, maintained numerically strong armored troops in their armies in peacetime years. In Great Britain, theoretical discussion of the future use of armored vehicles was encouraged above all else. It reached a high level. Much experimenting was done at that time.

In the German Army, awareness that battles could be won with the new weapon took hold only very late; thus only a very small tank corps existed at the end of World War I. Its soldiers were all the more confronted with questions of defense against tanks, and were able to gather by far the most inclusive theoretical and practical experience in this area. After Germany had lost the war, experience resulted in the awareness that the successful waging of military conflict was no longer conceivable without a satisfactory solution of the tank-defense problem. Yet because of the restrictions imposed on the German forces by the Treaty of Versailles, no practical results were to emerge at first. The development of, production of and equipping of the Reichswehr with special antitank weapons was forbidden. Thus in the first postwar years a broad theoretical discussion in the specialist literature and press took on much importance. In its course, numerous technical, tactical and organizational questions could be answered; they were important for the future development of antitank troops. A start was also made in using available means and possibilities to build up makeshift active and passive antitank defenses in the Reichswehr. Among the former were the infantry's mine launchers and the field artillery's guns. The latter consisted mainly of natural and artificial tank obstacles, a form of antitank defense that was seen as particularly important because of the small numbers of permitted and suitable weapons.

In the first half of the twenties, the development of an antitank gun had begun as part of the secret arming of the Reichswehr with weapons regarded as urgently needed. The gun was seen as the most vital prerequisite for successful antitank defense. On the one hand, tactical and technical experience gained in World War I favored it; on the other, the military understandably agreed on wanting a uniform weapon for the infantry. It should be just as suitable for tank and low-flying plane defense as for infantry support, which raised numerous problems. Only in the mid-twenties, because of the different needs of these tasks, was the final decision made to develop special guns for those purposes. Thus the 3.7 cm Antitank Cannon (3.7-cm-Tank) emerged, one of the first modern antitank guns, with all the characteristics of such a weapon. They included a long cannon barrel, spread mount and low silhouette. With it, the development of weapons technology in Germany first came to a definite solution. This was not true of the further development of ideas on tactics, structure and organization of the antitank forces. Here general principles developed until the mid-thirties. Among the most important results was the concept of antitank defense as a focal-point task of a special troop, at first called Panzerabwehrtruppe, renamed Panzerjägertruppe from 1940 on. This name was more closely linked with the purpose of carrying out antitank combat offensively. The subordination of the tank-destroyer troops was noteworthy. One part, the tank destroyer platoons and companies, belonged to the infantry. The tank destroyer platoons and companies in the armored and motorized units, like all the tank destroyer units in the divisions, corps and armies, belonged to the armored troops. In principle, this rule remained in effect to the end of World War II.

With the origin of special antitank guns at the beginning of the thirties, military arming in all large European armies, a competition began between the protective effect of armor and the destructive effect of armor-piercing weapons and their ammunition. Its development took place at ever-greater speed. Whoever neglected it, like the Germans at the beginning of the war, had to pay with setbacks and defeats. This development is somewhat comparable with that of fortress and naval combat. In the German Army, the search for a successful solution to antitank defense became a chief problem of waging war itself, involving all the branches of the Army and parts of the Luftwaffe. The tank destroyer troop was regarded as an essential part of this process. In short order, more effective antitank guns and vehicles were developed, manufactuired and delivered to the troops. This took up a considerable portion of the total military arming. Similarly, the basis of action, structure and organization of the tank destroyer troops changed during the course of the war.

It is not easy to determine and evaluate the success of the tank destroyers in concert with the tanks, artillery and other weapons. The material superiority of Germany's enemies in the realm of armored equipment can be seen in the fact that during the war the Soviet Union, the USA and Great Britain produced some 200,000 tanks and self-propelled guns. This fact allows German statistics to claim only secondary importance in terms of their success. The study of the history of the German antitank troops is interesting, though, and not only because weapons and principles of action were developed during the war which influenced the military after 1945.

The authors would like to thank retired Colonel Elser of Oldenburg, Mr. Hoppe and Mr. Simon of Berlin, and Mr. Thiede of Dresden for their assistance. Valuable help also came from the military archives in Freiburg, to whom we extend our thanks.

Freital, Spring 1998
Wolfgang Fleischer
Richard Eiermann

I. THE TWENTIES: THE FIRST MOTORIZED FIELD ARTILLERY

I. The Beginnings of Antitank Troops

The beginnings of the antitank troops must be dated at the beginning of the thirties. In January 1932 the Chief of the Army Command, Generaloberst Wilhelm Heye, approved the Reichswehr's second armament program. The goal was the creation of attaining the material prerequisites of the 21-division so-called A-Army by 1938. Now the conclusions drawn in the autumn of 1928 for the 16-division "Necessity Army" had a particularly advantageous effect in the area of antitank defense. The most important theoretical and practical provisions could be taken as given in 1932. In the realm of financial planning—always a problem area—there was also progress. But important decisions as to the armament of a future antitank troop had already been made at an earlier point, on February 3, 1925. On that day, during a conference of the Army command, the Technical Office and the Army Weapons Office, the development of a special gun mount, well suited to antitank use, for a 3.7 cm L/45 cannon barrel had been advocated. Among the other military requirements of an antitank gun was the possibility of being able to disassemble the gun into several loads. It was to have as low an overall height as possible, be no heavier than 250 kilograms, and penetrate 40 mm of armor plate at a range of 500 meters with an impact angle of 60 degrees. Its development had to be done under extreme secrecy, as the terms of the Treaty of Versailles in 1918 had forbidden the Reichswehr the development and availability of such a gun. Despite the constant lack of finances, the development and production of the antitank gun had been put in Urgency List 1 in January 1927. Just one year later, in January 1928, the first two test models

In January 1928 the first test models of the "3.7 cm Antitank Cannon" were finished. The gun weighed 330 kg and fired antitank shells with an initial velocity of 760 m/sec. Note the iron-tired spoked wooden wheels and the wide leather towing belts for manpower towing (on the spar).

The 3.7 cm Antitank Gun made by Rheinmetall, on a stiff wheeled mount, weighed only 175 kg and appeared at the end of World War I. Despite a number of defects, this early antitank gun was the starting point for further development in the twenties.

were finished. With equal intensity the Army Weapons Office promoted the development of a targeting scope, a 3.7 cm explosive antitank shell with tracer, ground fuze and brass cartridge case. In May 1929 thirteen guns were being built; the Army Weapons Office had already accepted five. The official designation of the antitank gun was "3.7 cm Antitank Cannon on Spread Mount".

No troop testing was done, for reasons of secrecy. The gun was instantly available if needed in case of war. Despite the early start and all the following efforts, at the beginning of September 1932, nine months after the end of the Reichswehr's second armament program, only 264 of the antitank guns were on hand. This was much lower than the planned supply. On November 20, 1932, the specified supply of 608 antitank guns for an army with 21 infantry divisions, three cavalry divisions and two mounted brigades fell short by 344 guns.

It was planned to equip every infantry battalion with two antitank guns. They were to be included in the 4th (machine gun) company, for which a fifth platoon was planned. For secrecy's sake it was designated "wooden gun platoon". No information is at hand about to what extent these conceptions had been realized in the expansion of the Army. It is known that with this structure the antitank guns would be in the front part of the infantry's combat order. At the regimental level there was scarcely a chance to train antitank reservists. The Reichswehr was obviously aware of the impossibility of these regulations and the necessity of having to strengthen antitank defenses in the foreseeable future. for organizational preparations had already been made. The important fact that the antitank guns had to be just as mobile as the tanks was already clear. To be able to make this happen, the "3.7 cm Antitank Cannon on Spread Mount" had to be adapted from horsedrawn to motor vehicle towing. On September 17, 1934 the Chief of the Army Command ordered the rebuilding of already finished antitank guns, which was done at the armories of the defense districts. The lower mounts gained swinging joints with springs; in place of the steel-tired spoked wooden wheels there were steel disc hubs with low-pressure pneumatic tires. Newly made guns were so equipped from the start.

With these technical changes the important prerequisites for the formation of a fully motorized antitank troop in the Army had been given in the mid-thirties. How far had the conceptions for structure and organization of these troops developed by then? Here basic changes from the 1932-33 concepts had been made. There were changes in the Infantry's antitank companies in the rifle regiments and antitank units of the divisions. The heavy companies or squadrons of the battalions in the rifle regiments (mot.) of armored divisions, and the reconnaissance units (except in the mountain divisions) had acquired antitank platoons. With this structure, these troops were to be better able to handle the special nature of mobile combat. Antitank units available to the higher troop command were established only when the war began as Army antitank troops.

Let us now turn to the infantry antitank companies (mot Z). Every rifle regiment had such a fully motorized unit for its protection against tank attacks. Thus the antitank platoons, previously intended for the battalions, were now combined at the regimental level. At the same time, the number of antitank guns in a regiment was raised from eight to twelve. The structure of an antitank company (mot Z) into four platoons, each with three 3.7 cm guns, allowed the commander, according to the combat situation, to divide the antitank platoons among the three battalions and withhold a reserve of three guns, or to apply the entire company together at a particularly endangered sector. It says in H.Dv. 130/5 "Training Manual for the Infantry, Volume 5, The Infantry Antitank

Structure of a Rifle Battalion of the Reichswehr, as of 1932

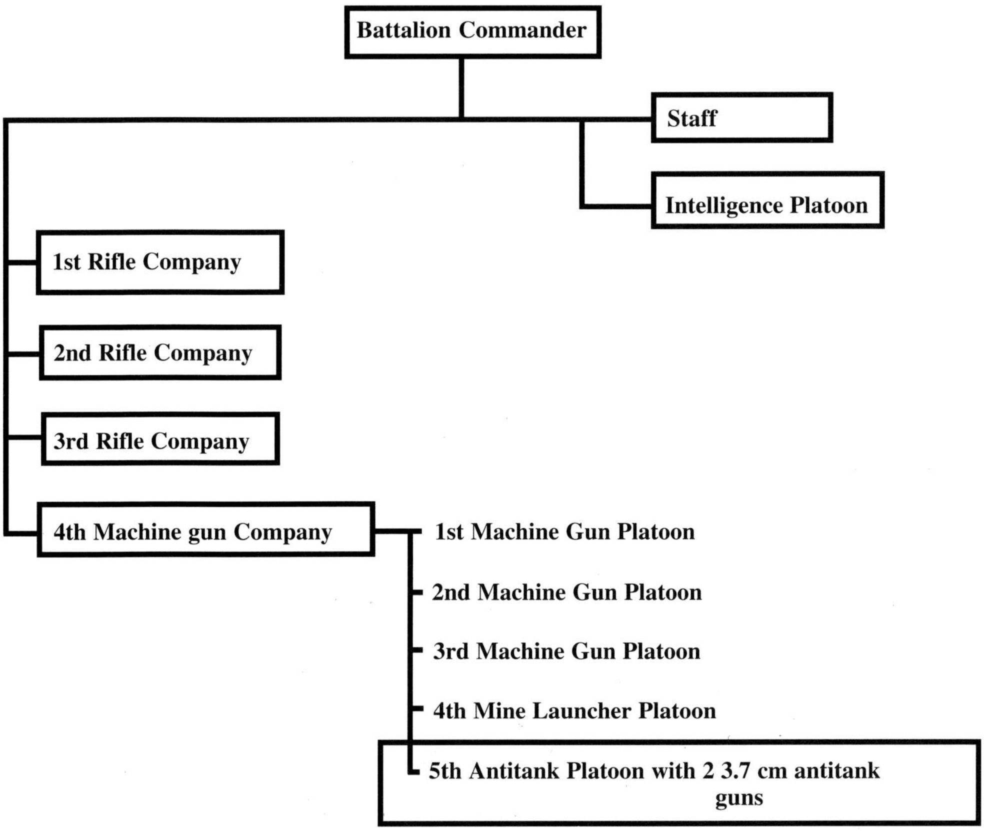

Dummy "antitank cannons", towed by horses or motor vehicles, existed in the Reichswehr. They were also called "wooden guns". Their use in drill and tactical training was a makeshift solution until sufficient numbers of "3.7 cm Antitank Cannons on Spread Mounts" were on hand.

Structure of an Infantry Tank-Destroyer Company c (of 12 guns) (mot.Z)
War Strength Report No. 184 c of November 1, 1941

Company Commander

- **Company Troop**
- **1st Platoon**
  - 3 3.7 cm Antitank Cannon L/45
  - 7 Medium gl. Vehicles (Kfz.12)
  - 3 Ammunition Trailers, one-axle (Sd.Anh.32)
- **2nd Platoon**
  - 3 3.7 cm Antitank Cannon L/45
  - 7 Medium gl. Vehicles (Kfz.12)
  - 3 Ammunition Trailers, one-axle (Sd.Anh.32)
- **3rd Platoon**
  - 3 3.7 cm Antitank Cannon L/45
  - 7 Medium gl. Vehicles (Kfz.12)
  - 3 Ammunition Trailers, one-axle (Sd.Anh.32)
- **4th Platoon**
  - 3 3.7 cm Antitank Cannon L/45
  - 7 Medium gl. Vehicles (Kfz.12)
  - 3 Ammunition Trailers, one-axle (Sd.Anh.32)
- **Supply Train**
- **Vehicle Repair Troop**
- **Baggage Train**

Total Strength
5 Officers
30 NCO
118 Men
12 3.7 cm
Antitank Gun L/45
12 Ammunition Trailer
(Sd.Anh.32)
23 Medium gl. Vehicles
(Kfz.12)

Company" of 1938: "Safety from tanks on the main battle line is to be striven for; it can be decisive. Dividing the infantry antitank company in action on the regiment's entire defensive front is best avoided when attacking possibilities for enemy tanks can be limited to certain areas of the terrain by natural and artificial means (barricades, mines). . . . The main task of the infantry antitank company is . . . assuring the protection of the main battlefield and the troops in action on it."

An interesting solution was found for the towed guns in the infantry antitank companies. They differed from those in the antitank units. For every gun there were two medium off-road-capable personnel cars (Kfz.12) with towing hooks. One was to tow the 3.7 cm antitank gun, the second towed the single-axle ammunition trailer (Sd.Anh.32) that went with it. The following considerations dominated: The infantry antitank companies seeing longtime service on the battlefield were necessarily more strongly exposed to the effect of enemy artillery fire. If the towing vehicles, being especially sensitive to fire, broke down, mobility was in danger of being lost. The availability of two medium off-road-capable personnel cars offered the possibility of keeping at least the gun and some of the ammunition supply mobile. Another reason derived from the fact that the German automobile industry was still in a crisis at the beginning of the thirties, and the lacking production capacity in individual firms could be evened out most easily by the production of as many types of towing vehicles developed from stock chassis as possible.These vehicles were also cheaper to produce than expensive special vehicles. The variety of models, adding up to eleven different manufacturers and types, was accepted in the bargain. Their insufficient off-road capability would prove to be a disadvantage.

In the reconnaissance units (t mot) of the infantry divisions there were antitank platoons with three 3.7 cm antitank cannons in the heavy squadrons. Their task was protecting their own advance troops against tank attacks.

The formation of motorized antitank units in the divisions was seen as a vital task in the formation of a future antitank troop with modern weapons and training. They were in the area of the Inspection of Motorized Troops. With their help, antitank defense was to be increased; they formed the reserve of the command. Heinz Guderian wrote in his book "Achtung Panzer!": "Now the task increased for it (the Inspection of Motorized Troops) of setting up quickly mobile, thus motorized antitank units for the command. All the Army's large bodies were given these units, their way of fighting in cooperation with tanks was developed, and thus the Army's defensive power against the danger of tanks was increased."

The cadre formations of the antitank units came from the Reichswehr's motor vehicle units, which from 1932 on had been formed into a motorcycle rifle, a tank and a dummy tank company. In addition, three vehicle units each had an antitank company, which had originally been planned for the three cavalry divisions. From these and the dummy tank companies there arose the antitank units. The meaning, which included a high degree of mobility, is shown by the fact that these units were the only fully motorized trops in the infantry divisions before World War II.

A first step in building up the antitank units was taken by the Army from the summer of 1934 to the end of 1936, whereby a multitude of material and personnel problems had to be solved. One example: The cadre units of Antitank Units 12 and 20 had been formed out of the Schwerin Half-Unit of Motor

Left page: A 3.7 cm antitank gun is seen during Reichswehr maneuvers in the mid-thirties. The three-piece upper shield could be folded down to decrease the overall height and make the gun easier to camouflage.

Above: An infantry antitank company (later infantry tank destroyer company) is reviewed. The first Kfz.12 tows the 3.7 cm antitank cannon with spread mount, the second tows its ammunition trailer (Sd.Anh.32).

Structure of an Antitank Unit (mot.Z) of an Infantry Division as of 1939

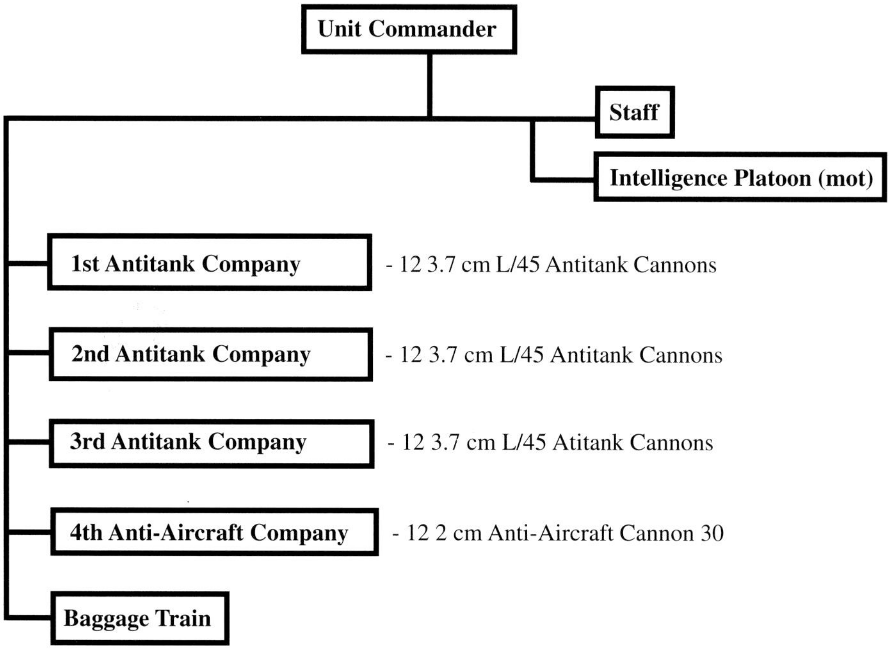

Total Strength
36 3.7 cm L/45 Antitank Cannons
12 2 cm Anti-Aircraft Cannon 30

Vehicle Unit 2 in October 1935. Antitank Unit 20 at first consisted only of the taff, intelligence platoon and two antitank companies. Antitank Unit 42 was formed of parts of Motor Vehicle Unit 5 (Vehicle Unit Würzburg B), and became the basis of Antitank Unit 25. The 3rd Company joined Antitank Unit 8 at the Neuhammer training camp in October 1936. Personnel assignments to other units followed.

Along with the deviations from the structure and specified equipment in the initial phase resulting from shortages of personnel, weapons, vehicles and equipment, the antitank units showed several structural differences that were based on the structure of the individual divisions. In general they were divided into staff, intelligence platoon and three antitank companies, but tank and mountain divisions were sometimes meant to have only two antitank units. This goal was attained by 1939 by all divisions of the 1st to 4th Waves and the armored divisions that existed when the war began. In addition, the antitank units of the 1st Wave had a 3rd or 4th (AA) company. The divisions of the German Army were equipped with antitank and anti-aircraft guns as follows when the war began in 1939:

The most important towing vehicle in the anti-tank units was at first the Limber Vehicle Kfz 69 (Krupp L 2 H 43 and L 2 H 143). Every platoon had a machine-gun troop with a light machine gun for close-range defense against infantry and low-flying planes.

The vehicles and guns of an antitank unit gather before marching out to a drill. In the foreground are dummy tanks of a dummy tank company. It was divided into three platoons of, at first, four vehicles each.

Division Type	3.7 cm L/45 Antitank Gun	2 cm AA MG 30
Infantry Divisions (1st-4th Waves)	75	12[1]
Mountain Divisions	48	12[2]
Infantry Divisions (mot)	72	12
Armored Divisions	48	12[3]
Light Divisions	54	12
Cavalry Brigades	21	12

Footnotes:
1. Only in first-wave infantry divisions.
2. Only present in the 1st Mountain Division.
3. No uniform equipping with AA companies.

The 3.7 cm Antitank Cannon with spread mount is seen in firing position during prewar maneuvers. It was the gun leader's task to choose the positoonso that the guns area of traverse (30 degrees to each side) could be fully utilized.

Among the special characteristics of the 3.7 cm Antitank Cannon were the high initial velocity of its shells (745 m/sec), the wide traverse field (60 degrees), the high rate of fire (up to 15 rounds per minute), the low height and the possibility of being towed quickly by a vehicle.

In the armored divisions, the 1-ton Demag D 7 Light Tractor (Sd.Kfz.10) replaced the Limber Vehicle (Kfz.69) because of its higher degree of mobility.

The antitank units in the infantry divisions uniformly possessed, from 1936 on, three antitank companies of three platoons, each with three, and later four, 3.7 cm Antitank Cannon L/45, 36 guns in all. This considerable firepower could be divided among the division's three infantry regiments in order to strengthen the 14th (antitank) companies there. But it was also possible to bring them into action together. It was stated in D 87 "Guidelines for Antitank Defense by All Weapons" of May 2, 1936: "The antitank troops of the high commander are the decisive means of shattering even large tank attacks. By using their mobility, they must intervene at the decisive place at the right time." It was further stated: "Division and splintering let the firepower of these antitank troops have an effect only insufficiently. Therefore their action generally takes place in united units." For the antitank units too, securing the main battle line against tank attacks became the main task.

The number of antitank units increased from 14 in 1934 to 53 in 1939. In case of war there were even 121, for the antitank units for the use of the higher troop command, as corps and army troops, then came to be set up. In the war structure of the field army there were ten antitank units planned, each with 36 3.7 cm Antitank Cannon L/45. Their task consisted of "strengthening the defensive power of threatened divisions or those fighting at focal points; for this they are subordinated on a case-to-case basis. Antitank troops of the corps and army troops can also be used to protect open deep flanks, backline connections and obstacle troops."

As towing tractors for the 3.7 cm Antitank Cannon L/45, the antitank units used the light off-road-capable one-ton truck (6x4), Tyle L 2 H 43 or L 2 H 143 (Kfz.69)

A gun crew was composed of the gun leader, gunners 1 to 4, and the driver of the Kfz. 69 Limber Vehicle. Another driver was added when the crew was equipped with the Kfz. 12.

In the interests of a surprise opening of fire by the antitank guns, during training there was already great emphasis on camouflaging the gun and tractor positions.

built since 1934. [p. 21] On this vehicle there rode, besides the driver, the five-man gun crew, and the combat supply of 180 antitank shells and 36 explosive shells was also carried. The vehicle became known by the designation of Protzkraftwagen or "Krupp-Protze".

In the antitank units of the armored divisions it very soon became clear that the off-road capability of the Protzkraftwagen (Kfz.69) was not always sufficient to follow the tanks into action. This was brought up in a discussion by commanders of antitank troops in War Zone X at the end of 1937. For the time being, though, supplying with new towing vehicles could not be counted on. Along with the ammunition urgently needed for firing training, numerous vehicles called for in the War Strength Reports were still lacking. There was also a shortage of trained drivers. Help was to be provided by the pre-military training of young men close to being drafted in the motor sport schools of the National Socialist Driving Corps (N.S.K.K.). In addition, it was hoped that "in the increasing motorization the . . . troops would receive sufficient replacements trained in driving."

Moving the unhitched gun during combat was to be limited to short distances. The reasons were: "Changing position by manpower over long distances eliminates, when fire is often opened immediately thereafter, calm and sure firing by the aiming gunner and makes ammunition replacement difficult."

The gun was the firing unit of the antitank companies; the gun leader ordered fire opened and was responsible for directing fire. Only in exceptional cases, for instance in ambushes, was that done by the platoon leader.

In firing training, special care was given to the cooperation of the gun crew during a firefight. Firing positions should be taken quickly and unobtrusively.

II. Shot Effect Versus Armor Plate

"The antitank troops with their antitank guns are the main providers of antitank defense by fire" (D 87 "Guidelines for Antitank Defense by All Weapons" of May 2, 1936, page 29). The main weapon of the antitank troops was the 3.7 cm Antitank Cannon L/45 (the designation of 3.7 cm Antitank Cannon on Spread Mount was no longer used from 1936 on). The important features of the gun were the single shot, the high rate of fire (15 rounds per minute), direct fire, and the large traverse field. The most important type of ammunition for antitank use until 1940 was the 3.7 cm antitank shell; its older form had a bullet weighing 0.695 kg., which was fired at an initial velocity of 758 m/sec. An antitank explosive shell with an initial velocity of 745 m/sec came into general use. This ammunition offered good hopes of success for accurate shooting at ranges under 800 meters. In D 228 "Training Manual for Firing Against Tanks" of June 20, 1936, it was stressed "that from 900 meters on, with increasing ranges, the hopes of success in fighting tanks grew much worse. From 900 meters on the percentage of direct hits under combat accuracy falls under 50% . . . and the trajectories go high over tank height." In fact, the limited range for direct fire gave the gun crew only very little time. Tanks that came up to firing positions at a speed of 12 kph could normally cover the 800 meters in four minutes. In that time it was possible to fire up to 60 rounds. The gun crews were drilled to prepare to make full use of their guns' rate of fire, and firing over 600 meters was called a waste of ammunition and reserved for only especially favorable combat situations. In training, sharpshooting at moving targets was given much attention. Good results were not lacking.

In one shooting test of Antitank Unit 20 (Schwerin, later Hamburg) at the Putlos firing range, 28 members could score 100 direct hits—to give just one example. Firing quickly and accurately was the one goal. And what about the armor-piercing effect of this gun's ammunition? With the 3.7 cm antitank

At the home barracks of the antitank troops, firing training with targeting ammunition (liner tube) was done. "Firing with targeting ammunition is the most valuable means of training the aiming gunners and involving the aiming and loading guners in firing activity."

shell at a range of 500 meters and an angle of 60 degrees, 29 mm of armor plate could be penetrated. That was too little in the mid-thirties, six years after the introduction of the 3.7 cm Antitank Cannon L/45. In France, where the slow-moving but more heavily armored tanks used for infantry support had the advantage, production of the D-1 medium tank had already begun in 1931. Its 40 mm front armor must be noted as an answer to the development of special armor-piercing guns. The competition between antitank defense, based mainly on the armor-piercing effect of their strongest weapons, and the effect of more and more improved protective armor was in action. The performance advantage achieved by the German Army thus decreased, a development that did not come as a surprise to the responsible parties in the Army Weapons Office. By the end of the twenties, antitank guns whose performance was better than that of the "3.7 cm Antitank Cannon in Spread Mount" then in production were repeatedly called for. A document from the Army Weapons Office/Weapon Testing Section IV of December 12, 1929 can be taken as an example that, to complement that gun, a "3.7 cm antitank cannon (K) in all-round firing mount" should be developed. A test model with L/64 barrel length was produced in 1930. Obviously, its performance was not good enough, for in the mid-thirties tha Army Weapons Office tested 3.7 cm antitank guns L/70 barrels. In firing 0.75 kg shells with caps, penetration results on armor plate were slightly above those of the weapon put into use by the troops. A comparison:

Penetration Results at an angle of 60 degrees at 1000 meter range

3.7 cm Antitank Cannon L/45	22 mm
3.7 cm Antitank Cannon L/70	24-25 mm

The increased performance was within limits and bore no relation to increased effort. Because of the longer barrel, officers of the antitank troops also expressed concern; it hindered off-road travel, its muzzle hit the ground and put the gun out of adjustment.

As a further possibility of improving performance, increasing the caliber was considered. This too was first considered at the end of the twenties. Information about when the development of the 5 cm antitank gun was begun is not available. Practical results of this kind led to a gun with spread mount and firing head. The

Penetration results for the 3.7 cm Tank Destroyer Cannon L/45 at an angle of 60 degrees and a plate firmness of 80-100 kg/mm²

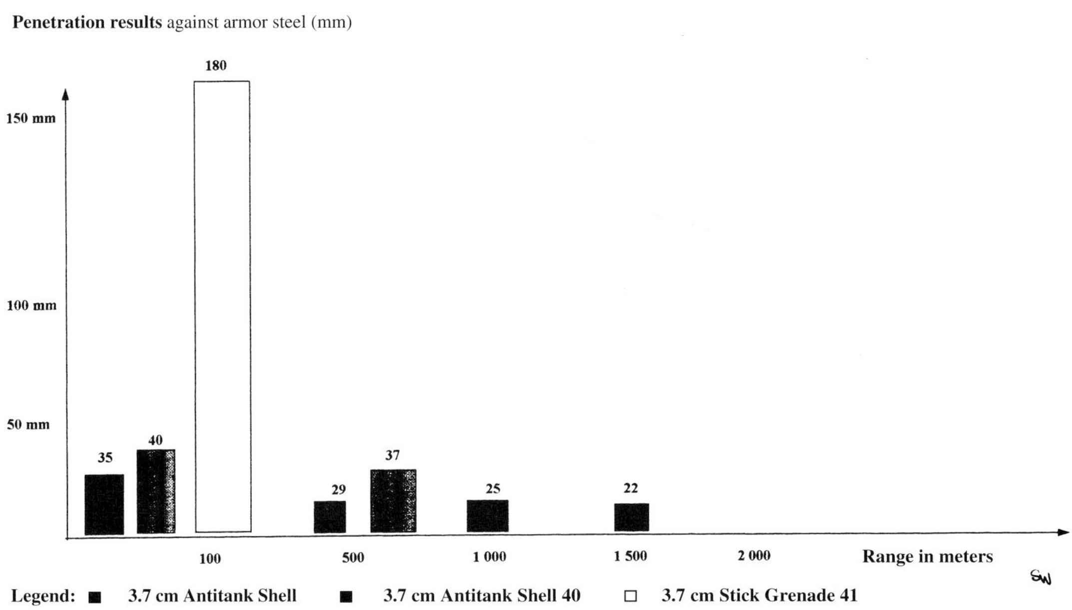

Ammunition of the 3.7 cm Pak
3.7 cm Pzgr.Patr.

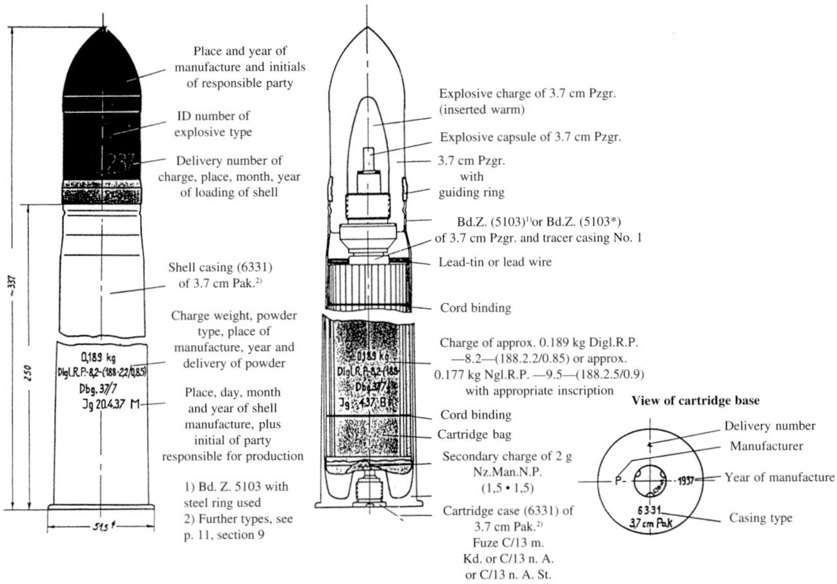

latter was used because of the greater weight (some 1200 kg) and was supposed to allow all-around fire. The testing of the 5 cm antitank cannon with spread mount and firing head is covered by the Army Weapons Office/Weapon Testing Sections IV and VI in the late autumn of 1937. Another antitank shell of 5 cm caliber was made at this time under the Inspection of Fortresses in the Army High Command. It was planned for use in casemates and turret mounts of fortresses. At a range of 500 meters it had a penetrating power of 62 mm of armor plate; at 1000 meters 51 mm.

None of the newly developed antitank cannons came into use by the antitank troops. This neglect was to be a serious loss in antitank defense during the war. As to the background, only suspicions can be had, as the written records of eyewitnesses include only very general statements (for example, Emil Leeb, retired General of the Artillery, Chief of the Army Weapons Office from April 15, 1940 to the end of the war, in the work "From the Armaments of the Third Reich", in Appendix 4 of Wehrtechnische Monatshefte, May 1958, Berlin-Frankfurt am Main, p. 36).

The new armament of thr antitank troops certainly would have been an additional burden in the tense armament situation in the latter half of the thirties. Related problems, though—as shown by the development of other weapons and equipment—were always solved as soon as the Army command recognized the need as urgently required. Did they become aware of this concretely? This question must be raised. From the Spanish theater of war, to which, according to a report of the Wehrmacht Office/Special Staff W of November 5, 1937, 202 3.7 cm Antitank Cannon L/45 and 146,600 antitank shells were delivered, there came very assuring reports as to the effectiveness of the gun. As early as March 20 of that year, the 8th Unit of the Army General Staff reported in a collection of technical experience from Spain that the "Tanks are presently inferior to the well-organized antitank defense". Obviously the impression of success with the 3.7 cm Antitank Cannon L/45 had not given the necessary impetus to the develpment of this weapon, and available test models of higher-performance guns had been discarded for minor faults. It would also be noteworthy that during the Spanish Civil War only tanks whose armor offered protection only against infantry weapons (16-22 mm) saw action. Under these conditions the axplosive antitank shell of the 3.7 cm Antitank Cannon L/45 could supply satisfactory effects even at 900-meter range.

In the prevailing conditions of the latter thirties, in addition to false evaluations of technical development tendencies in the relationship of tanks and antitank weapons, other basic considerations were involved. They can only be noted here with no guarantee of completeness. Linked to the conceptions of when a war would break out was the question of the Army's readiness for war. Were the quality and quantity of the military potential of possible enemies estimated correctly? This question must be answered negatively at least in reference to the Russian forces.

Without noticing the ever-clearer developmental trends, the development of antitank troops in Germany was advanced energetically. The large-scale production of the 3.7 cm Antitank Cannon L/45 reached considerable proportions in 1937. Every month some 120 guns were delivered. By the end of August 1938 their numbers were recorded as 8,449, a number that was to increase to 13,331 by May 1940. In comparison, France had some 5700 antitank guns in that month, Great Britain 600 to 700. This comparison alone makes it clear that on the German side the importance of strong antitank defense was not underestimated, whereby their own conceptions of the use of antitank guns in large armored troops was surely considered.

Along with the 3.7 cm Antitank Cannon L/45, with which the antitank companies and units were armed, the Army had another gun for antitank use, developed from the 8.8 cm anti-aircraft cannon. In 1938 the Army General Staff/Quartermaster General cooperated with the Army Weapons Office, Inspection 4 of the Luftwaffe Office and the Daimler-Benz AG firm of Berlin-Marienfelde to develop such a weapon, the purpose of which was first seen to be fighting against machine-gun nests in bunkers. The "eight-eight" was splendidly suited to such firing tasks. Its 10.2 kg armor-piercing explosive shells had a high initial velocity (810 m/sec). Firing tests on bunkers at 800- to 900-meter range gave a hit quotient with destructive effect of some 30%. In connection with the gun's great penetrating power (106 mm of armor plate at 1000 meters at a 60-degree angle), the Army saw good prerequisites for its use against bunkers and armor at long ranges. In 1938 two variations were tested, plus a test model with the barrel of the 10.5 cm anti-aircraft cannon. One was a partly armored 8.8 self-propelled mount on the chassis of the 12-ton Dbs8 Heavy Tractor. The

On a testing trip of a test command of the Army Weapons Office which was conducted from November 11 to December 2, 1937, a new 5 cm antitank gun with spread mount and firing head was taken along.

The 8.8 cm Anti-Aircraft Cannon 18 on a 12-ton Heavy Towing Tractor DB 9 (Sd.Kfz.8) was used as a tank-destroyer weapon, as seen in the 1940 French campaign.

other type was an 8.8 cm gun on a special trailer with a partly armored tractor. Both were no longer suitable for anti-aircraft use. A weight of 17,000 kg is listed for the self-propelled mount, with a firing height of about 2.60 meters. This naturally goes against the principles of use in the antitank troops, where special value was placed on good camouflage and low height in the interests of surprise firing. Despite all objections, after inspecting a test model at the Jüterbog training camp in the autumn of 1938, thirty 8.8 cm guns were ordered. This order was presumably filled, for when the French campaign began on May 10, 1940, three tank-destroyer units of the Army (No. 525, 560 and 605) were each equipped with twelve 8.8 cm antitank cannons (mot) ready for action. There was also an independent company with six 8.8 cm guns on self-propelled mounts.

Because of the 8.8 cm gun's great weight, it was absolutely necessary, in addition to the great mobility and readiness to fire needed for bunker and tank fighting, to develop a self-propelled mount. This resulted in a heavy and much too big vehicle, which was not satisfactory except for the performance of the gun. The idea of using self-propelled mounts for antitank use is thus not so new. In 1926 Fritz Heigl wrote about it in the "Pocket Book of Tanks" and, citing experience from World War I, commented that a "mobile defensive gun on tracks" capable of fast position changes was much more dangerous for tanks. In World War I the German side used 7.7 cm vehicle guns especially successfully in antitank defense. Therefore the vehicle guns were a valuable reinforcement for the poorly trained antitank defenses after the war. These were the Gun Vehicle 14 and 19 (Sd.Kfz.1), both at first fitted with a 7.7 cm gun. In a memo from the Defense Office to the Troop Office (No. 361/29 gKdos of March 25, 1929) it can be seen that between 1929 and 1932 a total of 120 7.7 cm vehicle guns were to be rebarreled in 7.5 cm caliber. This number may indicate the total number of guns on hand.

Structure of a Tank-Destroyer Company of 8.8 cm Flak 18
(of six guns) (mot.S)_,
War Strength Report No. 1146 of November 1, 1941

Company Leader

- **Company Troop**
- **Intelligence Staff**
- **1st Tank-Destroyer Platoon** with 2 8.8 cm AA Cannon 18 on 12-ton Heavy Tractor (Sd.Kfz.8) 1 Troop AA Vehicle (Kfz.4)
- **2nd Tank-Destroyer Platoon** with 2 8.8 cm AA Cannon 18 on 12-ton Heavy Tractor (Sd.Kfz.8) 1 Troop AA Vehicle (Kfz.4)
- **3rd Tank-Destroyer Platoon** with 2 8.8 cm AA Cannon 18 on 12-ton Heavy Tractor (Sd.Kfz.8) 1 Troop AA Vehicle (Kfz.4)
- **Supply Train**
- **Provision Train**
- **Baggage Train**

Total Strength
4 Officers
20 NCO
122 Men
6 8.8 cm AA Cannon 18 on
12-ton Heavy Tractor (Sd.Kfz.8)
1 12-ton Heavy Tractor
(Sd.Kfz.8)
3 Troop AA Vehicles
(Kfz.4)

A partly armored 8-ton towing tractor pulls an 8.8 cm tank-destroyer cannon. The large ground-combat shield and the shortened side spars (folded up) can be seen clearly.

In addition, the new development of "self-propelled mounts for antitank use" in the twenties was given much attention. This is noteworthy because of the meager financial means available for armaments. By 1931 no fewer than six test models of self-propelled mounts with 3.7 and 7.7 cm guns were made. These included makeshift and cheap, but also low-performance vehicles like the 25 HP WD Tractor of the Hanomag firm. Among the most expensive designs was Rheinmetall's third light tractor with a 3.7 cm gun in a pivot mount. From a 1929 memo of the Reichswehr's developmental program (TA No. 766/29 T 2 III C I gKdos"z" of May 24, 1929) it can be concluded that the end of troop testing of this self-propelled mount was expected in January 1931. In this developmental program it was stressed again that along with the hurried conclusion of the active developments necessary for the emergency equipping of the Reichswehr, "modern means of combat and command urgently had to emerge. Special emphasis was to be placed on tank, gas and aircraft defense. In the area of antitank defense, three self-propelled mounts were listed under III. Ideal Needs (Ideal Solutions):

A picture from France in 1940: the partly armored tractor pushes the gun into firing position, using its fromt towing hook.

1. Krupp Tracked Vehicle,
2. Horch Halftrack Vehicle,
3. Self-propelled Mount on the Light Tractor chassis.

The development, called for in 1932, of a light self-propelled mount for antitank defense on the

Another difference in the 88 cm AA Cannon is shown in this picture: a fast-loading box for three 8.8 cm shell cases, which could be fastened to the left side of the upper mount.

The partly armored 8-ton towing tractor was open to the rear to allow a quick debarkation of the gun crew. The picture dates from 1940.

The armor was limited to the engine compartment, driver and crew space, and the ammunition cases. The chassis itself was not protected. A disadvantage was the high bodywark of the partly armored tractor.

An Ehrhardt Type E-V/4 truck with a 7.7 cm anti-balloon cannon, seen during World War I. The German Army's few vehicle guns made important contributions to antitank defense in 1917-18. Experience gained then influenced the development of self-propelled antitank gun mounts after the war.

This Kw. 19 Gun Vehicle (Sd.Kfz.1) of the Reichswehr is on a training trip. The 11.25-ton vehicle reached a top speed of 20 kph. The 7.7 cm AA Gun 14 with L/27 barrel was mounted on it. These guns were rebarreled to 7.5 cm in the twenties.

For the Reichswehr, the few vehicle guns were a valuable reinforcement for antitank defense. The comparatively high speed of the trajectory (initial velocity 715 m/sec) and the penetrating power of the armorhead shell (30 mm of armor plate) allowed sufficient effect against even heavy tanks.

chassis of the small tractor failed from a series of technical problems and was abandoned. There followed a time that was characterized by a certain standstill in the area of development, manufacturing and testing of self-propelled mounts for antitank purposes. One exception was the aforementioned 8.8 cm self-propelled mount made in 1938. In addition, the Inspection of the Cavalry had begun experiments with 3.7 and 7.5 cm self-propelled guns on halftrack chassis. They are related to the development of the Army's antitank troops only insofar as a vehicle of the last type of this test series, the "Armored Self-propelled Mount III on 5-ton Medium Tractor Chassis" (Hkp 902), was put into action by the tank destroyer troops of the German Afrika Korps. The whole tangibly noticeable restraint in the development of self-propelled mounts for antitank use has a good reason, which must be seen in the production capacity of the German motor vehicle industry, which was still modest at that time. It was burdened with orders for the buildup of the armored troops; the preparation of a sufficient number of halftrack and fully tracked chassis for antitank use would have been unrealistic at that time.

The theoretical discussion of self-propelled mounts as a further promising weapon-technical concept for mobile antitank defense did not come to a stop. The proponents of self-propelled tank destroyers had justified doubts as to the correctness of the technical solution followed almost exclusively by the Army up to then, which was characterized by the separation of gun and towing vehicle. Their objections must be seen before the background of a hasty quantitative and qualitative further development of antitank weapons. Progress was made above all in the areas of speed, tactical mobility, armor protection and weapon effect. It is interesting that one of the protagonists of the tank, the later General Walther Nehring, in his 1935 writing "Antitank Defense", worked out the general fea-

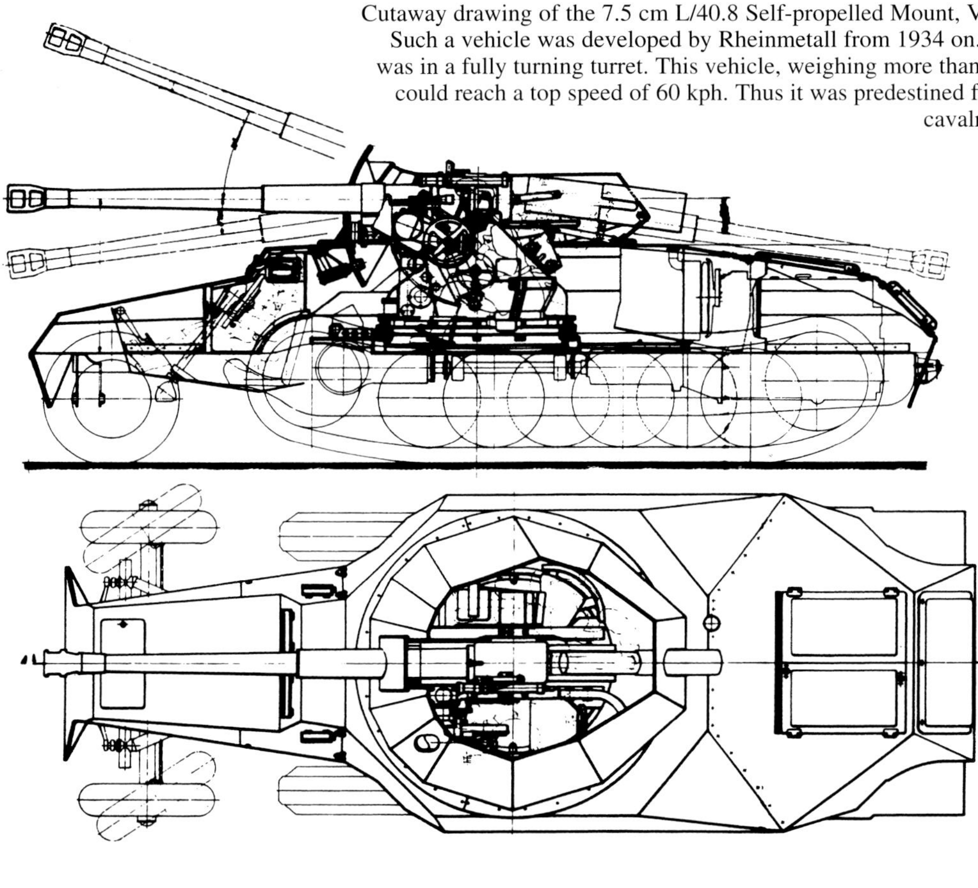

Cutaway drawing of the 7.5 cm L/40.8 Self-propelled Mount, Version 2. Such a vehicle was developed by Rheinmetall from 1934 on. The gun was in a fully turning turret. This vehicle, weighing more than six tons, could reach a top speed of 60 kph. Thus it was predestined for use by cavalry troops.

tures of "tank destroyers". They should have a lower weight, greater mobility and better observation suitability than tanks. A more effective armament was to make up for a lighter armor.

The need to set up special troop tank units with infantry-support tanks, advocated by other officers, tended to go in a very different direction. They could make special tank destroyers superfluous and "inspire the offensive spirit of the antitank troops anew, and thus also the infantry." The most thoroughly developed concepts were those of the later Field Marshal Erich von Manstein for an infantty assault gun. As is known, these considerations led to an assault gun that was to play an important role in antitank defense during World War II.

A striking agreement with the configuration of a self-propelled "tank destroyer" mount developed by Nehring was seen in the 1939 development by the Altmärkische Kettenfabrik of Berlin-Spandau of a test model 4.7 cm Antitank Gun (t) (Sfl) on Panzer I, Type B chassis. Of course the vehicle was a makeshift solution in every sense. Mustered-out tanks were armed with available Czech 4.7 cm Antitank Cannon L/43.4. In comparison with the German 3.7 cm Antitank Cannon L/45, this gun provided greater penetrating power. The following values were recorded:

Distance (meters)		**Penetrating power (mm)**	
	3.7 cm Pak L/45	**4.7 cm Pak (t) L/43.4 4.7 cm Antitank Shell 36 (t)**	**4.7 cm Antitank Shell 35 (ö) (umg.)**
100 meters	35	52	44
500 meters	29	47	41
1000 meters	22	40	34
1500 meters	20	35	25

All results apply to a striking angle of 60 degrees.

The 4.7 cm Antitank Cannon (t) Sfl was a small, light vehicle that was first used in the 1940 French campaign.

4.7 cm Antitank Shell 36 (t)

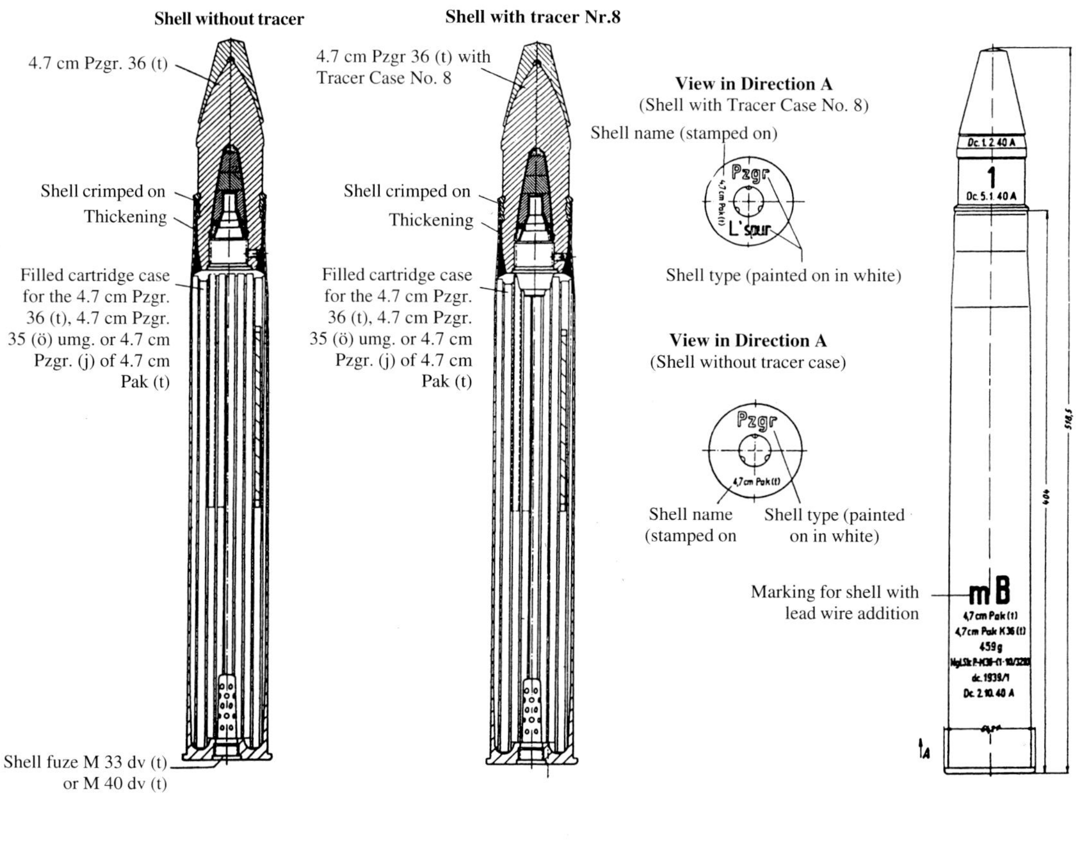

The total weight of Tank Destroyer I was listed as 6.4 tons, of which 0.595 ton was the weapon. The Skoda firm built it. At ranges up to 1000 meters, depending on striking angle, armor plate up to 55 mm could be penetrated—performance that was sufficient in battle against French tanks.

4.7 cm antitank shells were fired with an initial velocity of 775 m/sec. There was also explosive ammunition. Ranges up to 4000 meters were possible.

Along with Czech and Austrian ammunition, as of 1941 there were also supplies captured in Yugoslavia available. The crews of the antitank cannons were protected by a 14.5 cm three-piece shield.

The series rebuilding of Panzer I, Type B tanks into 4.7 cm self-propelled guns could begin only after the war had begun. It was planned to produce 132 self-propelled mounts between March and May 1940. The rebuilding actually ran until February 1941; 202 vehicles were prepared. On May 10, 1940 there were four Army tank-destroyer units, each with 18 4.7 cm Antitank Cannon (t)(Sfl) on Panzer I, Type B. Thus a further step was made in putting experience from World War I and knowledge from the extensive developmental work on antitank defense of the postwar era to practical use. Developmental trends in the realm of antitank guns outside Germany were watched carefully by the Army General Staff. They also reflected trends in tank design in the countries involved. Besides the already described 4.7 cm Antitank Cannon L/43.4 of the Czech armaments firm of Skoda, it was above all the French 47 mm Antitank Cannon mle. 1937 SA that gained renown in the latter half of the thirties. Its penetrating power at a range of 500 meters was a significant 50 mm of armor plate. The German side recognized the need to make contact again with the progress in performance made in other countries. Thus in 1938 a development contract was given to the Rheinmetall GmbH firm for a new and more powerful antitank cannon. The caliber of the 5 cm antitank cannon with spread mount and firing cap was to be maintained. But greater stability for the mount and higher penetrating power (60 mm of armor plate at 500 meters) were required. After testing, the gun went into series production at the end of 1939, and about 100 of the 5 cm Antitank Cannon were to be delivered in the first year. On May 1, 1940 two guns of the type were available, at the end of that month there were twenty. They were not used by the troops during the French campaign. A testing command of the Army Weapons Office led in early July 1940 to test firing on captured 70-ton Char 3 C tanks at Meussi—with success.

Despite that, the 5 cm Antitank Cannon,seen in present-day terms, was only a transitional solution that reached its performance limits in 1941, one year after its introduction. Of much greater significance for the technical development of Army anti-tank weapons

A self-propelled tank destroyer of Army Tank Destroyer Unit 521, which had been established as Antitank Unit (mot.) 521 in Defense Zone I on August 25, 1939 and rearmed with self-propelled guns in the spring of 1940. It saw service in France and on the eastern front, and was surrounded and wiped out at Stalingrad in January 1943.

A self-propelled tank destroyer in action. This picture again shows clearly the simple body and small dimensions of the vehicle.

The transfer of an Army tank destroyer unit with 18 Tank Destroyer I to the North African theater of war provided a valuable reinforcement in antitank defense for the German Afrikakorps.

A damaged Tank Destroyer I is taken away on a Tank Low Loader (Sd.Anh.115), which could carry up to ten tons. An 8-ton Medium Tractor KM m 11 (Sd.Kfz.7) is towing it.

Structure of a Tank Destroyer Company with 4.7 cm Pak (t)(Sfl) (of nine guns) (mot.S.) as part of an Army Tank Destroyer Unit

War Strength Report No. 1148 of November 1, 1941

- **Company Leader**
  - **Company Troop** — 1 Tank (MG) (Sd.Kfz.101), 1 medium gl PKW (Kfz.15)
  - **1st Tank Destroyer Platoon** — with 3 47.7 cm Pak (t)(Sfl) on Panzer I (Sd.Kfz.101), 1 Ammunition trailer (1-axle)
  - **2nd Tank Destroyer Platoon** — with 3 47.7 cm Pak (t)(Sfl) on Panzer I (Sd.Kfz.101), 1 Ammunition trailer (1-axle)
  - **3rd Tank Destroyer Platoon** — with 3 47.7 cm Pak (t)(Sfl) on Panzer I (Sd.Kfz.101), 1 Ammunition trailer (1-axle)
  - **Vehicle Repair Troop**
  - **Combat Supply Train I**
  - **Combat Supply Train II**
  - **Provision Train**
  - **Baggage Train**

Total Strength
4 Officers
22 NCO
78 men
9 4.7 cm Pak (t)(Sfl)
on Panzer I (Sd.Kfz.101)
1 Panzer I (MG)
(Sd.Kfz.101)

In D 249/1 "The 5 cm Antitank Cannon 38" of November 20, 1940, the gun was characterized as follows: "The 5 cm Antitank Cannon 38 (Pak 38) is a semi-automatic rapid-fire weapon with spread mount for vehicular towing. It serves to fire on armored targets . . . and living targets . . . in direct fire."

was the important progress in the realm of weapon and ammunition technology that marked the end of the thirties. To be named first of all were:

a. The development of hollow-charge ammunition for antitank use.

The development of hollow-charge ammunition under contract from the Army Weapons Office had been going on since 1930. At that time there was no exact physical explanation for the creation of the hollow-charge effect, nor could it be foreseen what increases in performance could be awaited. But they tried to evaluate the already empirically gained experience with the hollow charge for armor-piercing ammunition usable by the troops. The work progressed in three directions: the engineer hollow charge, the rifle shell for the paratroops, and the hollow-charge ammunition for big guns. The last-named area was of significance for the antitank troops.

In the Army Weapons Office, Major Schwenninger directed the development of hollow-charge shells. An initial result was the introduction on June 21, 1940 of "armor-breaking shells with great splinter effect" (= hollow-charge shells) for various guns of 7.5 cm caliber. The armor-penetrating power of the first hollow-charge shells was more or less equal to that of earlier explosive antitank shells. With a small striking angle for the shell and when fired from guns with low initial velocities, they were already superior to them at that time.

After short troop testing in North Africa, the hollow-charge shells were withdrawn. After the eastern campaign began in 1941, they achieved great, in some cases decisive importance for the antitank troops in the form of the stick grenade and the 38/HL grenade.

b. The development of high-performance weapons with conical barrels for antitank use

This weapon development was based on a patent from Carl Puff in 1903, pertaining to the use of conical barrels to increase the initial velocity of shells. In 1928 the engineer Hermann E.G.T. Gerlich began testing with such weapons of small caliber. His efforts to interest the Army Weapons Office in this expensive development remained unsuccessful at first. Only in the mid-thirties did extensive testing take place

The 3.7 cm Stick Grenade 41 for the 3.7 cm antitank cannon was a wing-stabilized hollow-charge shell that could be used in combat against tanks, as well as with good effect against living targets, barricades and protective walls. The picture shows, from left to right, an airtight ammunition container (7.65 kg), a 3.7 cm cartridge (0.7 kg), and the stick grenade (8.5 kg).

The shell had a diameter of 159 mm and a length of 737 mm. 2.3 kg of the 8.5 kg shell weight was that of the explosive charge. Favorable conditions for firing against tanks were ranges of 130 meters or less; they could be fired up to 700 meters at other targets.

with conical barrels of various calibers and appropriate ammunition. The stated purpose was to develop antitank weapons whose weighty shells were to have sufficient superiority in performance to be able to match the awaited development of tanks with shell-secure armor. The first weapon of this type was the 2.8 cm Panzerbüchse, with an interior barrel diameter tapering from 28 to 20 mm, shells fired with an initial velocity of 1400 m/sec, and a stated penetrating power of 40 mm of armor plate at a range of 500 meters. This value was 11 mm more than that of the 3.7 cm Antitank Cannon L/45. This weapon was introduced under the designation of Heavy Panzerbüchse 41. On Auigust 1, 1940 the Army Weapons Office reported the receipt of thirty weapons of this type. The projected monthly production goal (as of February 1941) was 200. Other antitank weapons with conical barrels were being developed at that time, of which those with calibers of 4.2/2.8 and 7.5/5/5 cm were introduced into the Army later.

The results of research on the development of ammunition for conical-barreled weapons was to be of great importance in upgrading the performance of the cylindrical-barreled antitank weapons being used by the troops. Until the spring of 1940, hard-core antitank shells for the 3.7 cm Antitank Cannon L/45 were more or less an offshoot of this work. The first shells with these bullets reached the troops in June 1940 and were used in the French campaign. The hard-core shell, weighing 0.368 kg, penetrated 64 mm of armor plate at 100 meters and 37 mm at 400 meters. At longer ranges their penetrating power was less than that of the usual explosive antitank shells. During the war, antitank shells were introduced under the designation of Antitank Shell 40 for almsot all antitank guns up to 8.8 cm caliber. Other countries copied this type of ammunition.

The 2.8 cm Heavy Panzerbüchse 41, weighing 223.3 kg in firing position, was an antitank weapon of the infantry and paratroops. The Tank Shell 41—a hard-core shell—was calibered down from 28 to 20 mm in the barrel and reached a maximum speed of 1404 m/sec. It was aimed by hand using an aiming arm.

The shell of the 2.8 cm Antitank Cartridge 41 was also called "flange shell" or "Kummersdorf shell" in the literature. It weighed 0.01 kg.

The 2.8 cm Heavy Panzerbüchse 41 on an infantry mount. The aiming scope behind a special armor plate can be seen clearly. Typical of this design are the shot-secure 27x4 air-chamber tires. A second version on a Light Mount 41 weighed only 118 kg. The lifetime of this gun's barrel was listed as 500 rounds.

III. The Antitank Troops in World War II

In September 1939 the Army had 11,200 3.7 cm Antitank Cannon L/45. The antitank troops seldom went into action against the small numbers of Polish tanks. Only 139 specimens of the highest-performance tank type of Polish origin, the 7 TP, existed in 1939. Its armor (at most 17 mm) offered no protection against 3.7 cm antitank shells. Thus the experience gained by the troops in the Polish campaign were limited more to individual technical problems. The swinging joints with springs on the lower mount were criticized. They proved to be too weak for the bad road conditions in Poland. This weakness kept turning up and was cured only in 1942 with the installation of the stronger suspension of the motor-towed 7.5 cm Light Infantry Gun 18. The troops also wanted a gun with a muzzle-flash damper like that of the Polish 3.7 cm Antitank Gun wz.36. Explosive shells were advocated. Their development was finished; their use had been canceled in favor of other types of weaponry. After the Polish campaign, a total of 94 3.7 cm Antitank Cannon L/45 had to be listed as total losses. This represented about half a month's production, which was listed for September 1939 as 202 guns. 1,793,000 shells had been consumed. While no antitank ammunition had been delivered in September, 594,000 and 327,000 shells had been produced in the next two months.

The number of 3.7 cm Antitank Cannon L/45 increased to 13,131 at the beginning of the French campaign on May 10, 1940. In all, Germany possessed about 15,000 antitank cannons, as follows:

13,131 3.7 cm Antitank Cannon L/45
20 5 cm Antitank Cannon 38
100 4.7 cm Antitank Cannon (t) (Sfl)

A Krupp L 2 H 143 (Kfz.69) one-ton limber truck (6x4) of the 1./Tank Destroyer Unit 90, 10th Armored Division, is seen during the 1940 French campaign. The antitank cannon is covered with its prescribed march-

Structure of an Infantry Tank Destroyer Company (of twelve guns) (horsedrawn)
War Strength Report No. 186 of October 1, 1939 (with Czech equipment)

Company Leader

Company Troop

1st Platoon
- 3 3.7 cm Tank Destroyer Cannon (t)
- 6 one-horse Mountain Cart 15 (t) (for ammunition)
- 1 locally typical two-horse ammunition wagon (substitute for Hf.1)

2nd Platoon
- 3 3.7 cm Tank Destroyer Cannon (t)
- 6 one-horse Mountain Cart 15 (t) (for ammunition)
- 1 locally typical two-horse ammunition wagon (substitute for Hf.1)

3rd Platoon
- 3 3.7 cm Tank Destroyer Cannon (t)
- 6 one-horse Mountain Cart 15 (t) (for ammunition)
- 1 locally typical two-horse ammunition wagon (substitute for Hf.1)

4th Platoon
- 3 3.7 cm Tank Destroyer Cannon (t)
- 6 one-horse Mountain Cart 15 (t) (for ammunition)
- 1 locally typical two-horse ammunition wagon (substitute for Hf.1)

Combat Supply Train

Provision Train

Baggage Train

Total Strength
5 officers
32 NCO
156 men
97 horses
12 3.7 cm Tank Destroyer Cannon 37 (t)
24 Mountain Cart 15 (t)
6 two-horse wagons

373 4.7 cm Antitank Cannon (ö) [o-umlaut = Austrian]
263 4.7 cm Antitank Cannon K.36(t)
1,205 3.7 cm Antitank Cannon M.37(t)
15,092 Antitank Cannons
The small losses in Poland and during the combat in the west (stated as nine guns for the period from November 1939 to February 1940) allowed the quick further expansion of the antitank troops. This was especially true of the units belonging to the Army. Here the totals on hand as of May 10, 1940 were as follows:
14 units of three companies each, of which seven (543, 559, 561, 563, 611, 652, 654) each had 36 3.7 cm Antitank Cannon L/45,
four (521, 616, 643, 670) each had 18 4.7 cm Antitank Cannon (t) (Sfl),
three (525, 560, 605) each had twelve 8.8 cm Antitank Cannon (Flak 18),
one company had six 8.8 cm Antitank Cannon (Sfl) (Flak 18).
Thus the statistics for antitank defense in the coming operations showed a significant potential

A burned-out self-propelled 8.8 cm gun on a 12 t DB 9 mount (Sd.Kfz.8), seen in the 1940 French campaign.

The Czech 4.7 cm antitank gun was used by the German Army in either horse- or motor-drawn form (4.7 cm Pak (t)/Kzg). There was also the 4.7 cm Antitank Cannon K 36 (t) casemate gun for use in fortifications.

power to be on hand. This is also shown by the following statistics: In 1940 the Allies had some 3400 tanks in western Europe. Thus there were four to five German antitank guns for every French or British tank. The significant numerical superiority of the German antitank defenses, though, did not achieve the hoped-for effect in this campaign. The most important reason for this must be seen in the fact that the French light tanks were already fitted with 40-45 mm frontal armor plate, and the considerably more heavily armored medium tanks had frontal armor of up to 60 mm. The British used infantry tanks with 60-80 mm armor. The gun crews of the 3.7 cm Antitank Cannon L/45 had only slim chances of fighting off tanks successfully. Surely their good training, already gained war experience, superior leadership and the courage and bravery of the soldiers made up for some of the technical inferiority. Local defensive crises and defeats, such as that of the 57th Infantry Division at the Abbeville bridgehead on June 4, 1940, were still sustained. First the 10,5 cm light howitzers and 8.8 cm Flak Cannon 18 and 36 had to be included in antitank defense. Thus just shortly after the end of the campaign it was stated in an experience report: "The insufficient penetrating power of the 3.7 cm Pak is known and is being eliminated." (Commander of the Army, Gen.St.d.H./Org.Abt.(I) No. 2980/40 geh. of 28 June 1940). They thought above all of the already mentioned 3.7 cm Antitank Shell 40, production of which began in the spring of 1940. It even had to be listed briefly in the category of decisive weapons and ammunition. The penetrating power and effect of this ammunition proved to be too meager, as its further development would show very soon. In addition, the meager effective shot range of the 3.7 cm Antitank Shell 40 had a negative influence on the tactics of combat against other tanks.

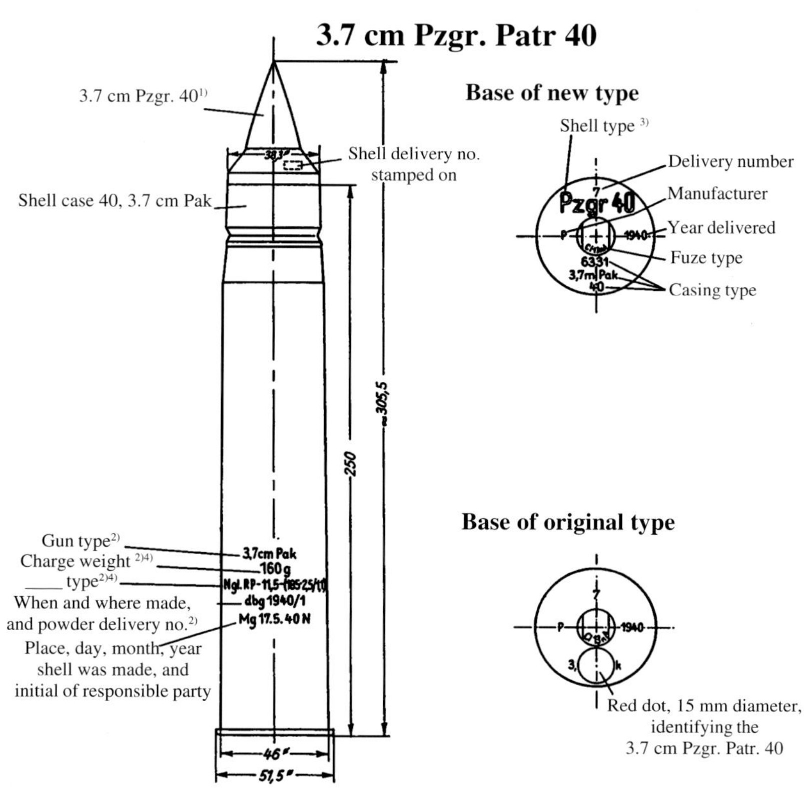

The 5 cm Tank Destroyer Cannon 38 weighed 986 kg in firing position and was too heavy and immobile to be effective. Antitank shells were fired with an initial velocity of 823 m/sec; antitank shells with cores reached 1198 m/sec.

A further increase in the effectiveness of antitank defense was anticipated by the Army from the new 5 cm Antitank Cannon 38, though on July 1, 1940 only 29 of the 0 series were available. Large-series production was to begin in July or August with 20 to 30 guns made per month. The introduction of further armor-piercing weapons was ahead.

Significant factors, by which the action of the antitank troops in the first war year could be characterized, were their mobility and speed, marked by the spirit of offensive action. This found visible expression in their nomenclature during the renaming of all antitank units as tank destroyer units on March 16, 1940 (General Army Information 353/1940 of March 21, 1940). The Infantry's antitank forces followed; they were called infantry tank destroyers from then on. The antitank cannons became tank destroyer cannons, and the self-propelled antitank cannons became tank destroyers.

There had been several attempts to rename the antitank troops as tank destroyer troops in the thirties. In August 1936 the use of the word "Panzerjäger" had been expressly forbidden, probably for fear that other countries could derive a conception of the action principles of the antitank defense from the name. The ban had little sense. In Issue 11 of the periodical "Kraftfahrkampftruppe" of November 1937, an unnamed author polemicized against the concept of antitank defense: "Psychologically, that is in its actual effect. . . the designation of 'Panzerabwehr' is not exactly a good choice, as purpose definition and destructive principle are not sufficiently expressed." In Issue 10 of "Kraftfahrkampftruppe" for 1938, the basic principles of antitank defense were stressed even more clearly: "The brutal attacking fury of the tank must be answered by a superior commanding spirit of the antitank forces and a cheerfully attacking force of unheard-of attacking verve and fanatical will to destroy." Their slogan was "Always ready to lurk, spring and destroy." In this article, which was published with the title "Spirit and Sense of the Antitank Weapon", the demands on a soldier of this troop were also sketched: "Along with the obvious command over their weapons, this task requires . . . courageous men

The Assault Emblem for Tank Destroyers

with strong nerves, well-trained bodies and personal energy . . . thus men with an outstanding attacking spirit!"

From a present-day point of view, the negative results of overstressing the offensive spirit of antitank combat in connection with the no longer sufficient performance of the 3.7 cm Tank Destroyer Cannon L/45 are obvious. It must be remembered that the antitank forces had by now become a target of the enemy attacking artillery and fighter planes. They found themselves playing the role of the machine gun in World War I. If they wanted to survive the heavy fire and air attacks that prepared for the tank attacks as unscathed as possible, they had to do it in well-built and -camouflaged positions. Their guns and towing vehicles were unarmored. Every attempt to change a position in order to react, if possible, against a focal-point gathering of attacking tanks, could mean their loss. There are various reasons why this did not result in a catastrophe in May and June 1940, during the French campaign. Along with the very quickly growing general superiority of the German combat forces was the lack of unity in the action of the numerically strong French and British tanks. Thus striking success was not gained. On the German side there were no large-scale defeats. This was to look very different a year later, when the attacks against the Soviet Union began.

A picture from the French campaign, in early June 1940, shows vehicles of an infantry tank destroyer company passing a group of French war prisoners and refugees.

The 3.7 cm tank destroyer cannon weighed 450 kg in firing position; the barrel was 1665 mm (L/45) long. Older barrels were made of several pieces (inner barrel with crimped-on mantle); newer barrels were made as complete barrels.

A presumably posed picture from the French campaign, May-June 1940, shows a 3.7 cm tank destroyer cannon in an open firing position, with a D-2 medium tank in the background.

An infantry tank destroyer company marches through a town in occupied France. In the foreground, a 2 cm Anti-aircraft Cannon 30, which was on hand in company strength in some tank destroyer units, stands guard.

A whole series of prewar conceptions about tank defense did not survive in practice. So it is stated in D 87 "Guidelines for Antitank Defense of All Weapons": "With its intervention in combat, the antitank troops draw the fire of the enemy tanks and their guarding weapon on themselves. . . . All troops not able to defend against tanks withdraw via taking cover or being motionless. . . ." Antitank defense had become the task of all and could no longer be schematicized.

IV. Stringent Tests

The time between the French campaign and the campaigns of 1941 was marked by further improvement of the weapons, ammunition, equipment and vehicle supplies of the tank destroyer units and troops. War experience gained earlier was evaluated and utilized in training. Striking changes in structure and action principles, though, did not result. Then as before, the rules recorded in D 87 "Guidelines for Antitank Defense by All Weapons" retained their validity.

In answer to a repeatedly voiced request to improve the off-road capability of the tank destroyers in the armored divisions, so that they could develop mobility comparable to that of the tanks, in 1940 the one-ton light off-road vehicle (6x4), Type L 2 H43 or L 2 H143, began to be replaced by the D 7 Light Towing Tractor (Sd.Kfz.10). Some guns were mounted on halftrack vehicles, thus creating improvized light self-propelled tank-destroyer mounts.

The vehicles issued to the infantry tank destroyer companies, some of which had gone into the war in 1940 equipped with stock trucks, were also upgraded. War Strength Report No. 184c of January 31, 1941 anticipated three varied means of equipping the infantry tank destroyer companies with towing vehicles: A: Kfz.12; B: Kfz.69; or C: one platoon with Sd.Kfz.10. Along with the introduction of the heavy Panzerbüchse 41, special tank destroyer platoons with four guns of this type were set up (War Strength Report 1147 of January 1, 1941). Five Kfz.69 or 1.5-ton light trucks saw towing service. There were also infantry tank destroyer companies with twelve guns and 18 M. 15 mountain carts, which had to be horsedrawn. There were 97 horses on hand for them. Some of these companies were equipped with Czech 3.7 cm Tank Destroyer Cannon M.37. In place of horses, some tank destroyer companies were issued French half- or fulltracy tractors in the spring of 1941. The UE 630 (f)—frz. Renault ue ammunition carrier was often seen.

Effective antitank defense took on a special value for airborne operations. For this purpose the Luftwaffe had received 45 3.7 cm Tank Destroyer Cannon L/45, adapted for parachute dropping, in April and May 1940. The army itself, according to War Strength Report No. 1141 (LL) of February 1, 1941, set up airborne tank destroyer companies. Each company had four heavy Panzerbüchse 41 and eight 3.7 cm Tank Destroyer Cannon L.45. The ground echelon was fully motorized with five Kfz.12 and 15 Kfz.69. A flying echelon was added for airborne action.

In February 1941, German troops took part in the combat action between their Italian allies and the British in North Africa. In this new theater of war, the insufficient performance of the 3.7 cm Tank Destroyer Cannon L/45 became clear once again. The broad battlefield and meager possibilities of camouflage compelled fire to be opened against attacking tanks at long ranges. The unlikelihood of scoring hits and the insufficient penetrating power of the shells opposed them. In part, this lack was made up for by introducing more of the 5 cm Tank Destroyer Cannon 38, but its penetrating power (47 mm of armor) was also insufficient.

The transfer of an Army tank destroyer unit with 18 Tank Destroyer I (4.7 cm Tank Destroyer Cannon (t)(Sfl) to North Africa gave the German Afrikakorps a weapon with great tactical mobility. Its penetrating power (4o mm of armor at 1000 meters), though, was also insufficient. The most important and effective German antitank weapon in North Africa was the 8.8 cm AA Cannon; its Antitank Shell 39 could pierce 88 mm or armor at 2000 meters.

Series production of the 5 cm Tank Destroyer Cannon 38 proceeded slowly. The great expectations of the spring of 1940 could not be fulfilled. Generaloberst Franz Halder noted in his diary on December 19, 1940: ""'Production problems with the 5 cm Pak will be overcome." By June 1, 1941 their numbers grew to 1047 guns. In the tank destroyer

A 5 cm Tank Destroyer Cannon 38 is seen in the North African theater of war.

The penetrating power of the 5 cm Tank Destroyer Cannon 38 soon became insufficient in North Africa. Firing was carried on there at long ranges. At 1000 meters the 5 cm shell with cap and hood pierced 51 mm of armor—too little for the heavily armored British infantry tanks.

In the German Afrikakorps the 8.8 cm AA cannon became the most important antitank weapon. It was no wonder, what with its noteworthy penetrating power (106 mm of armor plate at 1000 meters, 88 mm at 2000 meters). The guns were used effectively on offense and defense, and were fired from special trailers in critical situations.

companies there were thus only a few platoons with two 5 cm Tank Destroyer Cannon 38. To spare the weapons, they could be used exclusively against armored targets. The guns of the 3.7 cm tank destroyer platoons, with explosive shells, were to be used against living targets. The 5 cm explosive shells were kept for urgent exceptional cases, for self-defense. In a report by the Army High Command on December 7, 1940 it was stated: "Supplying with this ammunition is not guaranteed."

On June 1, 1941 there were 14,459 of the 3.7 cm Tank Destroyer Cannon L/45 in the Army. The gun came from the manufacturers in consistently large numbers and remained the most important tank destroyer weapon in 1941. A further increase of the numbers of tank destroyer cannons resulted from the takeover of 823 47 mm Antitank Cannon mle.37 SA-APX from French supplies. Like the 5 ccm Tank Destroyer Cannon 38, they were equipped with a spur wheel and used mainly in the tank destroyer companies of the infantry regiments. The German captured-goods designation was "4.7 cm Tank Destroyer Cannon 181(f)-frz.37 SA-APX". Large numbers of French 25 mm Antitank Cannon mle. 34 and 37 (= 2.5 cm Tank Destroyer Cannon 112(f) and 113(f) were also taken over, but they played a secondary role.

On December 25, 1940 a development [p. 55] contract was issued for a second series of self-propelled tank destroyer mounts. Again the 4.7 cm Tank Destroyer Cannon (t) was to be used. The available chassis were captured French Renault R-35 tanks. According to Halder's notes, the tank destroyer was reported on by the Army General Staff on February 18, 1941. Accordingly, 90 Renault tanks with Czech 4.7 cm guns were ordered for the Army tank destroyer units. In fact, between May and October 1941, 174 vehicles were produced. Even before the attack on the Soviet Union, Army Tank Destroyer Unit 561 re-

Gun cleaning: "Only careful handling and care of the device assure top performance and protect it from premature failure." (H.Dv.393) "The 3.7 cm Antitank Cannon" of January 20, 1940). This picture was taken in Tank Destroyer Unit 4, 14th Armored Division, in the spring of 1941.

This 5 cm Tank Destroyer Cannon 38 in firing position was photographed in France in the summer of 1940, though the gun was not utilized in combat there. The airtight shell cases for four shells, which existed in this form only for this gun, are typical.

ceived 18 4.7 cm Tank Destroyer Cannon (t) on Tank 35 R(f) without turrets. The self-propelled mounts did not prove themselves very well in this function, for on July 10, 1941 the Army Tank Destroyer Unit already received 3.7 cm Tank Destroyer Cannons (mot Z) again.

Considerations for developing heavy self-propelled mounts for use against tanks and bunkers were developed further. During a discussion with Hitler on May 26, 1941 it was decided to develop both a self-propelled mount for the 12.8 cm Cannon L/61 and one for the 10.5 cm Cannon L/52. For the former, two chassis developed by Henschel in March 1941 for the VK 3001(H) tank were used; for the latter, two modified Panzer IV chassis. Only in 1942 were they tested by a tank destroyer troop under the designation Armored Self-propelled Mount V and IVa. There was no series production. The forerunner to this development was the 8.8 cm Tank Destroyer Cannon (ex-AA Cannon 18) on 12-ton tractor chassis, which was still in service with a tank destroyer company in 1941.

A noteworthy initiative was developed by the Army Weapons Office in the area of ammunition development, in order to modernize the German and captured tank destroyer cannons then in service. After the 3.7 cm Antitank Shell 40 was introduced in 1940, the combination of ammunition components for this gun was changed. They included:
120 antitank shells,

A welcome reinforcement for the Army tank destroyer troops was the French "Canon de 47 antichar SA-37". Ther 1070 kg gun fired 1.7 kg antitank shells with a listed initial velocity of 855 m/sec.

30 Antitank Shell 40,
100 explosive shells.

The new ammunition was also supposed to be available for the 5 cm Tank Destroyer Cannon 38. Generaloberst Franz Halder noted in his diary on February 18, 1941: "5 cm . . . with Antitank Shell 40 pierces 120 mm (aromr plate)(equipping with 10% intended)."

Officially, the 5 cm Antitank Shell 40 was introduced only on May 22, 1941 (AHA Ag.K. / In 6 (III/VIIIun.)No. 1745/41 geh.). Its penetrating power at 10-0 meters was actually 130 mm, reduced at 500 meters to 72 mm of armor. The ammunition supply for the 5 cm Tank Destroyer Cannon was composed of the following:
150 antitank shells,
40 Antitank Shell 40,
30 explosive shells.

In addition, the Antitank Shell 40 was introduced for the Czech and French antitank cannons in use by the Army at almost the same time.

In the summer of 1941 the Germans believed they were ready in terms of weapon technology for competition with the more numerous antitank weapons of the Red Army. Along with the tank destroyer units and troops in the divisions, 13 to 14 Army tank destroyer units were concentrated in the east. Only incomplete data on the actual strength of the Russian antitank weapons were available. Reports had spoken of 10,000 antitank weapons. It was not known that there were more than 18,000 of them. The further technical development of Russian antitank

Large numbers of French antitank guns were captured. A temporary equipment description (D 337) for the gun appeared on February 28, 1941, but a handbook for the ammunition (H.Dv. 481/177) came out only in June 1942. This picture was taken near Warsaw in the spring of 1941.

Captured French antitank guns were revised according to German action principles. This included a makeshift spur wheel to make it easier to move the gun by manpower. There were also a 4.7 cm Antitank Shell 40 (penetrating 70 mm of armor plate at 500 meters) and a 4.7 cm Stick Grenade 42 (penetrating 180 mm of armor at 100 meters) introduced.

4.7 cm Pzgr. Patr. 40 (f)

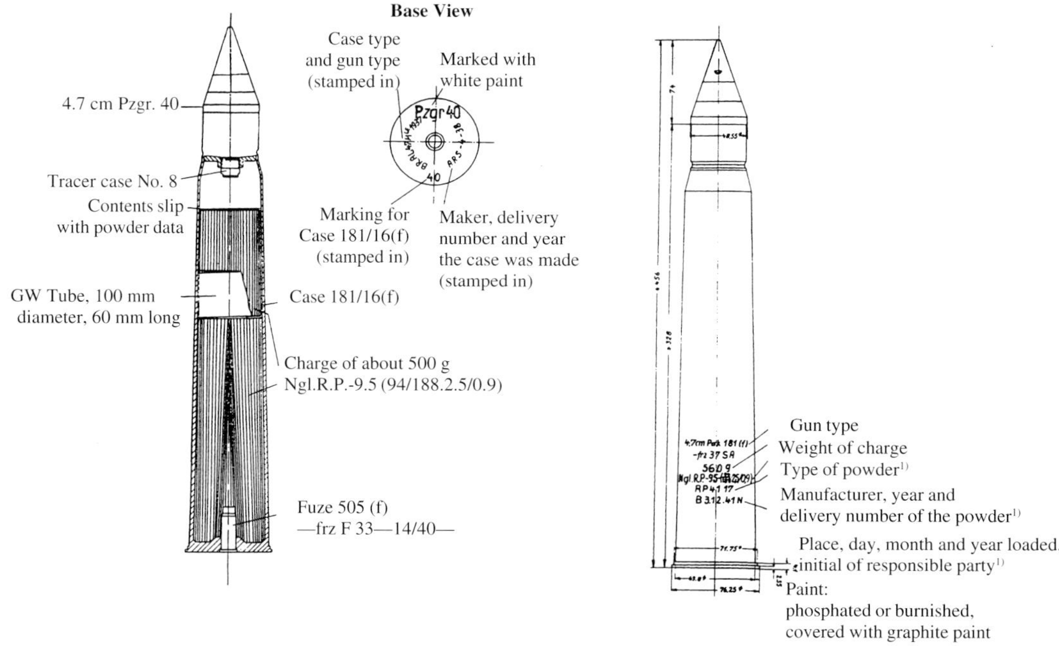

weapons was completely concealed from the Germans, except for a few reports from the 1939-40 winter war between Finland and the Soviet Union. Surprises were built in. The Army's tank destroyers were to face stringent tests.

Self-propelled tank destroyer mounts made by the troops took many forms to combine firepower and mobility effectively. In the picture is a 3.7 cm tank destroyer cannon on Demag D 7 one-ton light towing tractor (Sd.Kfz. 10).

3.7 cm guns were often mounted on one-ton Krupp L 2 H 143 limber trucks (Kfz.69), as here in an armored reconnaissance unit after the French campaign. The armored Ford-Marmon-Herrington next to the self-propelled mount is interesting.

The appearance of enemy armored vehicles had to be expected at any time. Thus early recognition of tank threats was very important. The effect of the surprise factor could be lessened, an important prerequisite for successful antitank defense.

The price of a 3.7 cm tank destroyer cannon was listed at 5730 Reichsmark. Its manufacture too 900 work hours. With one barrel, 4000 ro 5000 rounds could be fired.

SS tank destroyers of the Waffen-SS bring a 5 cm tank destroyer forward. From an experience report about the use of this gun in the Balkans in the spring of 1941 it appears that good results were also achieved with 5 cm explosive shells.

A 3.7 cm tank destroyer cannon lies in waiting. Between the spars are the shell cases for twelve chells, typical of this gun. There were also carrying cases for the ammunition.

V. 1941-42—The Tank Destroyer Troops Reorganized

It is not difficult to select individual passages from the many available reports to tell of the shock that the German soldiers experienced from their first meeting with heavy and ultra-heavy Russian tanks after June 22, 1941. First we have an excerpt from a portrayal by a war correspondent of Propaganda Company 612 on the defensive combat of an infantry division near Grodno on June 23 and 24:

"Loud motor rumbling from all sides—clouds of dust rise up all around us, the steel waves of tanks roll in simultaneously from three sides. Our breath stops from excitement. . . . The sun is already low on the horizon. . . . New attacks break forth from several directions. Assault wedges that are meant to penetrate weak positions. And then the cannon barrels rise above the horizon, a high turret becomes visible, a gigantic tank body. Tanks! Giant tanks such as we have never yet seen! Giants of steel stamp over the slope toward us! Russian 52-ton tanks with 15 cm guns! Crippling fear strikes us. Then the Pak guns are turned around, our fire bursts from all their barrels, but the light armor-piercing weapons can do nothing here. The shots bouncs off the mighty steel walls like rubber balls. . . . The antitank troops fight with wild intensity. The tank is their deadly enemy. They let it come on to the shortest ranges, fire coldbloodedly, as they have learned, at its weakest points. Fire till the armor plates glow from mighty hits and the borings of the antitank shells. . . . Before the last man sinks over the gun, he fires the last shot."

Somewhat less dramatic and marked by his typical factuality are the entries of the Chief of the Army General Staff, Generaloberst Franz Halder, in his war diary:

"June 24, 1941: New heavy tanks!

June 25, 1941: A few facts about newly appeared Russian tanks: Weight 52 tons, frontal armor 37 cm (?), side armor 8 cm, weapon 15.2 cm K and 3 MG, crew 5 men, speed 30 kph, action radius 100 km. Defensive possibilities: 5 cm Pak penetrates under the gun turret. 8.8 cm apparently penetrates on the sides too (Still doubtful). Another new type is reported. . . ."

Here he spoke of the KW-1 and 2 A heavy tanks and the T-34 medium tank. The two models were on hand in the Red Army in 1861 examples at the beginning of the combat between Germany and the Soviet Union, and constituted some 105 of its complete supply. A special commission of the Army High Command was hastily sent to the eastern front and examined Russian tanks shot down by Army Group North. On June 27, 1941 they presented a temporary report, followed by "Instructions for Fighting the Heavy Russian Tanks (50t)". The following bits of information about the possible success of armor-piercing weapons were offered:

1. 5 cm Tank Destroyer Cannon 38 with Antitank Shell 40—penetration possible up to 400 meters.
2. 4.7 cm Tank Destroyer Cannon (t) with Antitank Shell 40—penetration at ranges up to 200 meters.
3. 8.8 cm AA Cannon 18 and 36 with Antitank Shell 39—penetration at ranges up to 1000 meters.

A 3.7 cm gun of Tank Destroyer Unit 44, 1st Mountain Division, is firing in combat against bunkers.

A tank destroyer unit with mixed equipment is seen on the eastern front in July 1941. At right is a limber truck (Kfz.69) with 3.7 cm tank destroyer cannon, at left a towing tractor (Sd.Kfz.10) with 5 cm tank destroyer cannon.

The lack of suitable towing vehicles compelled infantry tank destroyer companies again to take the field with horsedrawn guns. If. 9 grenade-launcher cars were often used as limber vehicles. Infantry tank destroyers are passing a 1933 model Russian T-26 tank in June 1941.

These pictures are symbolic of the meager effect of German tank destroyer troops in the summer of 1941. Russian KW-1 44-ton heavy tanks first rolled over the guns, flattening them; then the tank crews carried on their destructive work among the towing vehicles. From then on the 3.7 cm cannon was nicknamed the "Army Door-knocker".

The 3.7 cm Tank Destroyer Cannon L/45 was no longer mentioned in these temporary instructions for antitank fighting. It was, as stated in a report about experiences in tank fighting in Tank Destroyer Unit 561: "powerless against the T-34, for the antitank shells slide off the sloping surfaces. . . . The KW tanks did not have such a favorable shape, but were so heavily armored (80-120 mm) that no shell penetrated."

Along with very effective armor protection, the T-34 in particular had superior off-road capability, as was portrayed in a further experience report: "It made special tactical measures of defense necessary." Departing from previous concepts, the 3.7 and 5 cm antitank cannons ignored longer ranges and concentrated on bringing the guns into action surprisingly from ambush positions. The troops at the front had to be ready to be rolled over by the tanks. Thus the use of tank-cover pits and ditches was recommended. For the tank destroyer guns, good cover and camouflage were important. Shots at tanks were to be taken at closest ranges and from cover. Also, hasty advance moves of the tank destroyers practiced in attacks according to past training and action principles under fire from Russian tanks and artillery caused unnecessarily high losses and belonged to the past.

In this context, a comparison of statistics is revelatory: In the 1940 French campaign there were four or five antitank guns per enemy tank, but at the beginning of the eastern campaign a much less favorable ratio existed—a Russian tank for each one of their guns.

The reports on the ineffectiveness of the 3.7 cm Tank Destroyer Cannon L/45 piled up during the autumn and winter of 1941. The infantry's trust in the tank destroyers assigned to it was shaken. There were cases of panic when Russian tanks appeared. The tank destroyers had to accept heavy losses of personnel and materials. Between June 22, 1941 and April 10, 1942 3540 of the 37.7 cm guns alone were

A self-propelled 3.7 cm tank destroyer mount of Tank Destroyer Unit 4, 14th Armored Division, seen on the eastern front in the summer of 1941.

After a Russian fighter-plane attack, a driver grimly looks at his "tank destroyer". This picture clearly shows the left gun spar on the left side of the vehicle.

Another makeshift solution for the sake of mobility was the 3.7 cm tank deestroyer cannon on the UE 630(f) ammunition carrier—frz. Renault UE. These vehicles, taken from French supplies, were issued to some tank destroyer units as towing vehicles.

In the (armored) gun battalions of the armored divisions, 3.7 cm tank destroyer cannons were mounted on the Schützenpanzerwagen (Sd.Kfz.251/19). The vehicle shown here has been hit by artillery fire; the wounded men seek shelter behind it.

A 5 cm Tank Destroter Cannon 38 with UE-630(f) ammunition carrier—frz. Renault UE—to tow it. The towing vehicles proved to be too sensitive under combat conditions and often broke down.

A different solution. Here a captured Russian Artillery Tractor 630(r) - russ. Komsomoletz - is towing a 5 cm Tank Destroyer 38 gun.

For the Russian campaign an independent company of the army tank destroyers was given 8.8 cm self-propelled guns. The achievements of the guns against heavily armored targets were good. The disadvantage was the high, often poorly armored body.

In view of the superior mobility of the Russian T-34 tank. the mobility of the German antitank defenses was decisively important. All resources were utilized. Here a French UE ammunition carrier tows a 5 cm Tank Destroyer Cannon 38.

Part of a horsedrawn infantry tank destroyer company with 3.7 cm tank destroyer cannons. The IF 9 grenade-launcher carts used as limbers can be seen clearly.

lost. This practically equaled the annual production of 1940 and 1941.

On December 15, 1941 the General High Command V. Army Corps thoroughely questioned the effectiveness of the 3.7 cm Tank Destroyer Cannon L/45. Success was gained only against British infantry tanks, which began to appear on the eastern front. At 150-meter range their side armor could be pierced. The 88th Infantry Division reported on March 23, 1942: "The 3.7 cm gun is insufficient for fighting the enemy's tank types that he now brings onto the battlefield. . . . The infantry's inclination toward tank panic cannot be overcome by means of training alone if it is not quickly given sufficient numbers of a weapon with which it can fight off enemy tanks with a hope of success."

An attempt to modernize the 3.7 cm Tank Destroyer Cannon L/45 consisted of the introduction of the 3.7 cm Stick Grenade 41. The 8.5 cm hollow-charge shell with a diameter of 160 mm could pierce 180 mm of armor plate. But fighting tanks was possible only at the "suicidal close-combat range" of 100 meters. In an experience report of the 1st Infantry Division it was then estimated: " Firirng the stick grenade requires more nerve, like close combat against tanks." Besides, loading the stick grenades into guns in position was difficult (Report on combat experiences, Gen.St.d.H./ Gen.d.Inf. I a No. 1700/42 g of August 1 1942).

Despite the not very cheering combat experience, as of early June 1942 there were still serious considerations by the Army High command as to giving the 3.7 cm Tank Destroyer Cannon L/45 with stick grenades a future place in antitank defense. It was even intended to put the gun back into series production, delivery of which had ended with 15 guns in

Ammunition of the 5 cm Pak 38

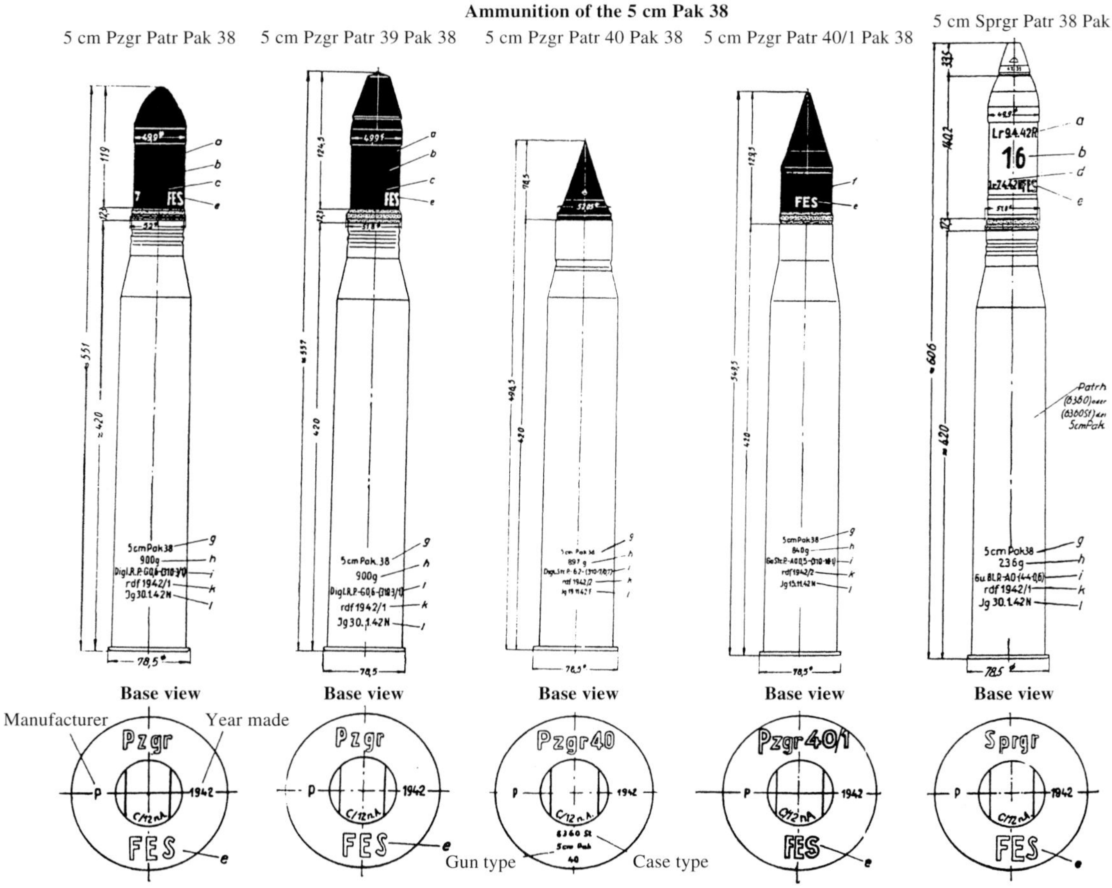

Penetrating performance of the 5 cm Tank Destroyer Cannon 38 at an angle of 60 degrees and armor plate firmness of 80-100 kg/mm^2

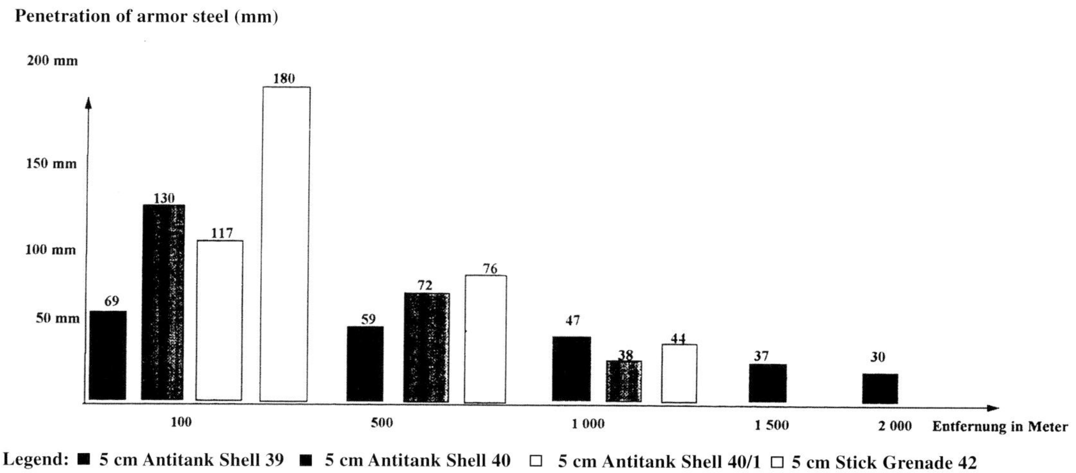

March 1942. Only on August 29, 1942 did the Army High Command finally decide to give up the 3.7 cm Tank Destroyer Cannon L/45. In the justification it was stated: "The weapon is no longer usable as a Pak (even with stick grenades it is just a makeshift help). Continuing its production only for use as an infantry assault gun is not justifiable." By November 1, 1944 the numbers continually decreased to 1309 pieces, the greatest numbers of which were in the tank destroyer replacement and training units of the replacement army.

The situation was not much better for the 5 cm Tank Destroyer Cannon 38, which had meanwhile been classified as a medium antitank gun. The effective range of this gun, 400 meters, was to little to be able to guarantee the troops protection from tank at-

This 5 cm tank destroyer cannon is out of the fight. The cost of making the gun amounted to 8000 Reichsmark. 1800 work hours were needed before it was turned over to the Army Weapons Office. The barrel's life span was listed as 4000 to 5000 rounds.

Structure of a Machine gun Company c (mot) of an Infantry Division (mot)
War Strength Report No. 161 c of November 1, 1941

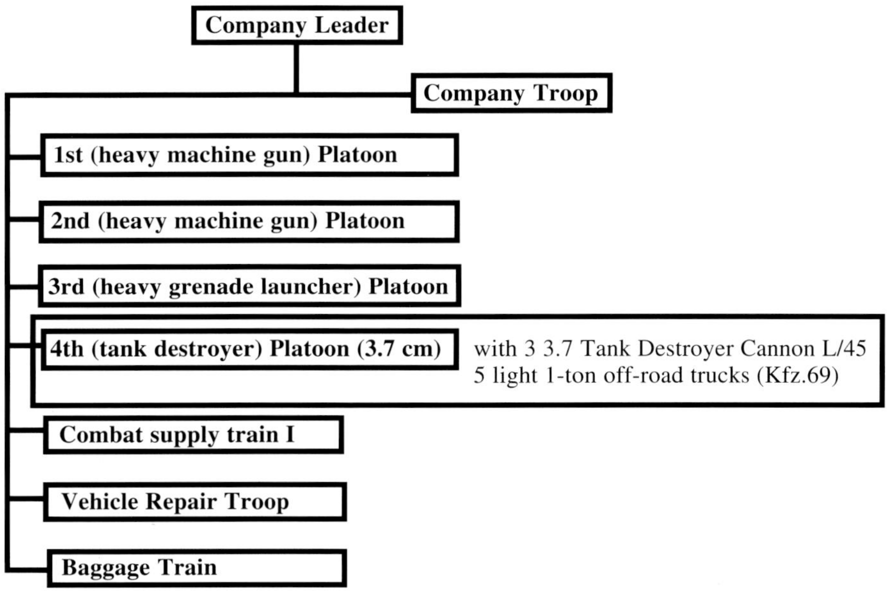

tacks. This was reflected in the losses too: Between December 1, 1941 and February 28, 1942, 269 Tank Destroyer Cannon 38 were lost. In a teletype the Army High Command estimated on Jnue 3, 1942, "that the 5 cm Tank Destroyer Cannon 38 shows too little performance in comparison to its high weight. . . ." They wished that production would be shifted to the new 7.5 cm tank destroyer cannon as soon as possible. Yet for the second half of 1942, higher production of the 5 cm cannon had to be arranged, so as to make up for the great lack of medium and heavy tank destroyer cannons (on May 1, 1942, about 2900 guns). A monthly quota of 300 guns was striven for. In 1943 it came to an end. In a report on August 14, 1943 it was said: "Despite good success, justification of the 5 cn Pak's presence in future combat must be questioned." On November 1, 1944 there were still 967 guns of this type on hand.

The justification of the 5 cm Tank Destroyer Cannon 38 actually remained limited for a year, from June 1940 to June 1941. With the appearance of modern Russian tanks, it no longer met its requirements. The gun is a classic example of wrong estimations by the military, here especially in the development of the relationship between offensive and defensive weapons, with the result that the troops were given weapons with insufficient performance. As for another antitank weapon, 178 of the 2.8 cm heavy Panzerbüchse 41 were present with the troops when the eastern campaign began. Through its favorable power-to-weight ratio (weighing 134 kg in firing position) and small dimensions, it could make an impression and was thus especially suited for use by the infantry tank destroyers. Disadvantages were the high wear and tear on the barrel (life span 250-300 rounds) and the great need for of tungsten and other scarce materials in ammunition production. Armor piercing was possible at ranges [p.72] under 100 meters, but the effect of the shots was too meager and seldom put a tank out of commission. On November 1, 1944 there were still 883 of them on hand, 473 of which were to be scrapped for lack of ammunition.

Important experiences and encouragement of further development of technology and tactics for the tank destroyer troops came in from another theater of war in 1941-42: from North Africa. Here operations to date in the broad, tank-favorable landscapes had shown overwhelming success in the use of heavy tanks. In August 1941, after the end of offensive operations in Cyrenaica, British countermeasures were expected. To be able to oppose them successfully, antitank defense in particular was to be strengthened. Requests were made of the Chief of Army Equipping and the Commander of the Replacement Army by the organization unit of the Army High Command for the German Afrikakorps for:

1. 5 cm tank destroyer cannons for the complete r armament of the tank destroyer units of the 15th and 21st Armored Divisions.
2. Rearming all light infantry gun platoons in the armored divisions with 5 cm tank destroyer cannons.
3. Rearming one 3.7 cm tank destroyer platoon of each heavy company in both machine gun battalions and full rearming of Tank Destroyer Company 8 of the 21st Armored Division.
4. Creating a reserve supply of 20 5 cm Tank De stroyer Cannon 38 and 20 Heavy Panzerbüchse 41.

Beyond that, it can be assumed from the note of August 17, 1941 in the war diary of Organization Unit III that, because of the unique terrain in North Africa "a fast tank defense on self-propelled mounts" was considered absoluteny necessary. Makeshift solutions were to be created quickly by mounting German 5 cm tank destroyer or Russian 7.62 cm field cannons on trucks or tractors. Twenty self-propelled guns were planned, and were to be sent to the German troops in North Africa after testing.

Nine vehicles with the 7.62 cm Field Cannon 296(r)—russ. 36—were ready at the end of 1941. There was also a platoon (with two guns) of Tank Destroyer (Sfl) 7.5 cm Cannon L/41on armored 5-ton tractor chassis, available as a development of the Army's cavalry; from these guns a good penetrating performance at ranges up to almost 1500 meters was expected. In fact, that range 59 mm of armor plate

The 2.8 cm Heavy Panzerbüchse 41 was used in Infantry Panzerbüchse troops. Some infantry tank destroyer companies had individual platoons with these high-performance but very expensive weapons. The production price was about 4500 Reichsmark; the life span of the barre! was about 500 rounds.

Against the T-34 medium tank the tank destroyer troops had chances of success with their 5 cm Tank Destroyer Cannon 38 only at ranges under 100 meters. It was more effective to let the tanks go by and fire from the side or the rear.

Captured Russian Field Cannon 36 were taken to Africa to strengthen antitank defense there. The German captured weapon designation was 7.62 cm Field Cannon 296 (r)—russ. 36. At a range of 1000 meters they could penetrate 67 mm of armor plate.

could still be pierced. The preferential supplying of the German rikakorps with high-performance antitank weapons was repeated in 1942, when it had to be realized there too that the 5 cm tank destroyer cannon could no longer meet its requirements.

In northwestern France, where certain numbers of army units were always stationed in anticipation of an invasion, the rearming of tank destroyer units with captured Czech, Belgian and French weapons was increased. For example, the High Commander West was directed in the spring of 1942 to set up horsedrawn infantry tank destroyer platoons according to War Strength Report 182, each with three 4.7 cm Tank Destroyer Cannon 818(f)—frz.37 SA-APX. A hundred guns with 15,000 antitank shells were made ready. On March 24, 1942 another 24 weapons in 4.7 cm caliber and 264 in 2.5 cm caliber were assigned. This arming with captured guns, by now mostly obsolete, rwas connected with the heavy weapon losses of the tank destroyer troops on the eastern front. Their effectiveness remained limited, even when Czech and French stick grenades were introduced for almost all tank destroyer cannons.

What typified the development of the Army's tank destroyer troops in the period from June 22, 1941 to the spring of 1942? The first meeting with the numerically superior tanks of the Red Army produced a condition of shock. The tank destroyers were the most important part of the antitank defense. Suddenly it was seen that they were overwhelmed with this task. Their meager efficiency took on a particular bitterness through the extensive ineffectuality of the German tanks in combat with the Russian tanks. In addition, the almost complete arming of the field artilery with howitzers limited their ability to share in effective antitank defense to ranges under 500 meters. The infantry was only insufficiently equipped with antitank weapons or means of fighting tanks. Here close-range tank fighting, seen until then as a type of last-ditch defense, quickly gained importance. In many places it was the only possibility of fighting off Russian tanks. The principle stated in 1936 in D 87 "Guidelines for Tank Defense by All Weapons", "For the main battle line, safety from tanks is to be striven for," could no longer be maintained. Now the facts—the overwhelming role of the tank on the battlefield and the poor effect of their own antitank weapons—forced a step-by-step rethinking. If they succeeded in stopping attacking tanks in the depths of their own defenses, that counted as success. To be sure, the German troops in 1941-42, when they were forced onto the defensive, could not form especially deep battle lines because of the broad extent of the front in the east. Besides, the superior off-road capability of the Russian T-34 upset all German conceptions about tank-safe terrain. The fact that there were no serious defeats in 1941-42 was because the Russian leadership at that time was not yet able to use their tank forces effectively. On the other hand, the German forces had the strategic initiative and could compensate for defeats in some sectors of the front.

What conclusions were drawn for the further development of the tank destroyer troops?

1. Modification of structure, command and action principles for antitank defense. This process was compelled to change among the troops and was already in progress.
2. The numerical strengthening of the tank destroyer troops:
   a. Through the use of captured antitank [p. 75] guns and field cannons in the tank destroyer units and troops—a temporary solution.
   b. Through the increase of monthly production figures for the 5 cm Tank Destroyer Cannon 38 and the hastened large-series production of new gun types.
3. The further technical development of antitank weapons. Here the following trends were seen:
   a. The creation of light antitank weapons for use on the front lines by the infantry tank destroyer companies.
   b. The development of heavy tank destyoyer cannons (mot Z) in 7.5 and 8.8 cm caliber for use in the tank destroyer units of the divisions, armies and the Army itself. They were supposed to allow successful antitank action at ranges of 1000 meters and more.

A 3.7 cm tank destroyer cannon is loaded onto a 500 kg Army sled (Hs.3).

c. The lack of suitable towing vehicles, the insufficient mobility and readiness to fire of towed tank destroyer cannons, and the lack of armor protection, gave the development of self-propelled tank destroyer mounts a particular importance.

d. The development of fully armored tank destroyers armed with high-performance guns in the manner of assault guns, such as were used since the spring of 1942 by the Army's assault artillery.

The grim reality of winter war in the east: a 3.7 cm tank destroyer cannon is provisionally loaded onto a sled made of tree trunks. One can no longer speak of tank destroyers.

In the winter of 1941-42 the tank destroyer troops lost much equipment on the eastern front, and it could not be replaced quickly by newly-made higher-performance guns. Thus the obsolete 3.7 cm gun continued to dominate in the spring of 1942.

During 1942 the 7.5 cm tank destroyer cannon was to become the most important and best-berforming gun of the tank destroyer units. Through its use on self-propelled mounts in particular, it was able to increase the efficiency of the tank destroyer troops again.

VI. Stronger Weapons, Revised Tactics

In the Army High Command, they clung to the 3.7 cm Tank Destroyer Cannon L/45 for an unusually long time. This fact was based on the desire to have a light and mobile antitank weapon on hand for the direct protection of the infantry. The insufficient penetrating power of the 3.7 cm cannon brought these efforts to an end. Another light antitank gun, the 4.2 cm Light Tank Destroyer Cannon 41, was available since December 1941. The Army Weapons Office had received five of them in November. The gun had a conical barrel similar to that of the 2.8 cm Heavy Panzerbüchse 41, combined with the mount of the obsolete 3.7 cm weapon. In firing position it weighed 560 kg, which was within the bearable limits for moving by manpower. With the 4.2 cm Antitank Shell 41, 101 mm of armor could be pierced at 100 meters and 67 mm at 500 meters. These impressive values were bought at the price of high barrel wear and tear (life span 500 to 1000 rounds) and a considerable need for tungsten for the hard-core ammunition. In 1943 the lack of tungsten compelled the dismantling of large supplies of this ammunition to regain the heavy metal. In May 1942 the production of the 4.2 cm Tank Destroyer Cannon 41 was halted. There were 136 of the guns in the army. They were used in the infantry tank destroyer companies of the mountain and infantry divisions, as well as the Luftwaffe's paratroop tank destroyers. By November 1944 the supply was down to 41 guns.

Traditional antitank guns, whether with cylindrical or conical barrels, were not a long-term solution to the need for an infantry antitank weapon. Further development led to two fully new weapons, the 8.8 cm Rocket Launcher 43 and the 8.8 cm Rocket Panzertbüchse 54, which were available from 1943 on.

Let us now turn to the medium and heavy guns. The monthly production of 5 cm tank destroyer cannons could be increased. For the autumn of 1942 it was planned to produce 400 to 450 guns. But consumption also remained at the high level of up to 270 guns.

The 7.5 cm Tank Destroyer Cannon 41 saw service in only small numbers. The manufacturing cost was listed as 15,000 Reichsmark, and 2800 work hours were needed to build a gun. The conical barrel (75-55 mm) endured about 1000 rounds of 7.5 cm Antitank Shell 41 HK, which had an initial velocity of 1220 m/sec.

The use of the 5 cm Tank Destroyer Cannon 38 was only worth using with the 5 cm Antitank Shell 40, which penetrated 130 mm of armor at 100 meters. The hard-core ammunition for this gun was in production until the war ended.

Just after the first firing tests at Russian tanks in June 1941, the Army Weapons Office had given contracts for the development of heavy 7.5 cm tank destroyer cannons with cylindrical and conical barrels. It was typical of the urgency of the developmental work that in July the production of 300 raw barrels was ordered, although the design had not achieved any tangible form at that time. Early in November the testing of several new tank destroyer cannon models took place at the Hillersleben firing range. Yet it was clear too all involved parties that the delivery of significant numbers of guns could be expected only in the spring of 1942. The lack of heavy tank destroyer cannons in the tank destroyer troops was to be made up by various makeshift solutions.

One of the first of these makeshift solutions was the 7.5 cm Tank Destroyer Cannon 97/38, which reached the troops early in the summer of 1942. Here barrels from captured French mle.1897 cannons had been combined with mounts of the 5 cm Tank Destroyer Cannon 38. To avoid stress for the mounts, the barrels were fitted with effective muzzle brakes. At first, mainly captured Polish and French ammunition was used, but except for the explosive shells, they were soon replaced by German-made hollow-charge ammunition. With them, 70 mm of armor could be pierced regardless of the range (7.5 cm Shell 15/38 HL/A(f)). The last 7.5 cm Shell 97/38 HL C(f) to be delivered penetrated 100 mm. For the 7.5 cm Tank Shell (p), 58 mm at 500 meters and 45 mm at 2000 meters are listed. In the autumn of 1942, barely 1600 guns of this type were on hand. A small series of 150 7.5 cm Tank Destroyer Cannon 97/40 were built in the end. The only difference was that the mount was identical to that of the 7.5 cm Tank Destroyer Cannon 40. The two models were used by tank destroyer platoons of two guns, which were [p.80] included as partial units in individual companies of tank destroyer units. They were classified at first as heavy, later as medium tank destroyer cannons. On February 26, 1943, combat experiences with the "Heavy Tank Destroyer Cannon 7.5 cm (f)" were reported by Fast

Unit 290: "Between 200 and 800 meters, T-34 tanks could be fought with good success." Further advantages were noted as the good effect against infantry attacks, the low firing height, and the easily adjusted traverse and elevation. A noticeable disadvantage was the lack of tracer ammunition, which resulted in heavy ammunition consumption. In a report from Army Group North, 12 to 24 rounds were said to be needed to shoot down a tank. In any case, the lack of a semi-automatic breech had a negative effect on the rate of fire. Another disadvantage was the jumping of the gun when fired, which required new aiming. Besides, hand-firing often failed—very typical features of such a makeshift solution. With the high series production of the 7.5 cm Tank Destroyer Cannon 40, the remaining guns were turned over to infantry tank destroyer companies. In 1945 there were small numbers of them in a few fortress Pak units.

Further makeshift solutions deserve to be noted in detail because of their importance in Army antitank defense. They include the 7.62 cm Tank Destroyer Cannon 36 and 39 plus the Field Cannon 296(r)—russ.36— and its variants of the same caliber. All of these were guns that could be captured in large numbers in the first weeks of the eastern campaign, and that were especially suitable for antitank defense on account of their ballistic characteristics. With the 7.62 cm Field Cannon 296(r)—russ.36— the loading chamber had to be fitted to the length of the 7.5 cm Tank Destroyer Cannon 40 shell, and the barrel was fitted with a muzzle brake. As of February 1942 the 7.62 cm Tank Shell 39 red was delivered, with which 80 mm of armor could be pierced even at a range of 1000 meters. [p. 81] For the field cannon, this value was 67 mm under the same conditions, while the Tank Destroyer Cannon 39 attained 71 mm.

In reference to the reuse of Russian field guns, the message that the Chief of the Army General Staff sent to all army commands in the east on August 5, 1942 (Oberkommando des Heeres /Chef d. Gen.St.d.H. Org Abt.III No. 7864/42 geh.) is of particular interest:

A 7.5 cm Tank Destroyer Cannon 97/38 used by a horsedrawn infantry tank destroyer company. The gun was a temporary thing. With the Polish shells originally used, 61 mm of armor could be pierced at 500 meters.

"The Russian 7.62 cm field gun had attained the best success after being reworked as an antitank gun for reuse on the German side. . . . The gun is already being planned today for issue to a series of German troops. The equipping of further troops is being planned.

"Of decisive importance for the reuse of the weapon is sufficient supplying through capture. Thus I request that the commanders of the troops consider the securing of this costly weapon and the prompt sending on of the captured pieces.

"For reuse, particularly the following types are considered:

—7.62 cm Light Field Cannon 36 Type 296(r) (especially with cast mount)

—7.62 cm Light Field Cannon D Type 296(r).

(signed) Halder"

Accordsing to available data, the Army Weapons Office gave a contract for a one-time rebuilding of a series of 900 Russian field cannons. Of them, 129 used the Field Cannon 39 (= 297(r)). The basis for this was the Führer's decision of August 18, 1942. In August 1944 19 more tank destroyer cannons were assembled from parts. Of the total of 919 Tank Destroyer Cannon 36 and 39, 564 were used to arm self-propelled mounts. In March 1945 there were still 165 guns of this type on wheeled mounts.

It can be seen from the experience reportsd from the eastern front that at ranges from 200 to 1400 meters the armor of all tanks, especially the T-34 and KW. could be pierced. The gun stood firm when fired, the rate of fire was judged to be sufficient, and the accuracy was also evaluated as good. An advantage was the availability of armor-piercing ammunition with tracers. Criticism went only to the heavy smoke production when firing, and the fact that because of the frontal weight of the barrel, the traversing machinery was very hard to operate. This decreased the chances of success in combat against fast-moving tanks. Thus on the eastern front in 1942 there was the paradoxical situation that the most effective weapons available for use by the Army's tank destroyer troops against Russian tanks were Russian-made guns. This fact makes clear the large gap that the German weapons technicians had to overcome.

The fact that attacking tanks could involve antitank defenses in a firefight at ever-growing distances forced a further development of antitank weapons, so that they could intervene in the fight at the greatest possible distance. For this, the Germans planned weapons of 7.5 and 8.8 cm calibers. The development of 7.5 cm antitank guns had been begun in 1938, but this work had been given priority only after the debacle of antitank defense in the east. In November 1941 the Army Weapons Office had tested the new

In the heavy platoons of some infantry tank destroyer companies too, the captured Russian 7.62 cm Field Cannon 296 (r)—russ. 36—could be found.

The Russian 7.62 cm Division Cannon 36 was captured in large numbers by the German Army and quickly gathered to be reworked as antitank guns. As the Tank Destroyer Cannon 36, this gun outperformed the Russian original in armor penetration by 17 mm.

The 7.62 cm Division Cannon 36 was also designated F-22 in the Red Army. It weighed about 1.6 tons in firing position and had shot ranges up to 13,600 meters.

In the German Army the Division Cannon was used unchanged as 7.62 mm Field Cannon 296 (r)—russ. 36— by some light artillery units of the divisional artilery as well as tank destroyer companies.

As the 7.62 cm Tank Destroyer Cannon 36 (r), the gun proved to be comparable to the German 7.5 cm Tank Destroyer Cannon 40 (penetrating 92 mm of armor at 500 meters).. The production expenditure was limited. The barrel's life span was given as 6000 rounds. This picture from the winter of 1943-44 shows such a gun (recognizable by its low shield) towed by the Tracked Tractor East (R.S.O.).

canons at Hillersleben; two of the models wre of 7.5 cm caliber. The first was a gun made by the firm of F. Krupp AG, which had a conical barrel (7.5/5.5 cm). In April and May 1942 a single series of 150 guns was produced. The official designation was 7.5 cm Tank Destroyer Cannon 41. With the 7.5 cm Antitank Shell 41 H.K. (initial velocity 1220-1260 m/sec), 167 mm of armor plate could be pierced at a range of 500 meters. A soft metal shot, introduced because of the tungsten shortage, brought it down to 78 mm. Front testing of gun and ammunition was entrusted to Army Tank Destroyer Unit 561, which could record much success during the fighting near Rshev in July and August 1942. Its companies had a mixed lot of four 5 cm Tank Destroyer Cannon 38, and four 7.5 cm Tank Destroyer Cannon 41. Russian tanks were shot down as they approached their own main battle line. Despite this, a general introduction of the gun did not take place.

The second gun was developed by the firm of Rheinmetall GmbH and designated 7.5 cm Tank Destroyer Cannon 44. In February 1942 the first weapons could be delivered. Despite their weight (1425 kg), which was considered too high, and some problems with the ammunition, the Army Weapons Office decided to give a contract for large-series production of the Rheinmetall design. The gun was given the final designation of 7.5 cm Tank Destroyer Cannon 40. With the Tank Shell 39 it could penetrate 91 mm of armor at a range of 500 meters, at 2000 meters it still pierced 63 mm. With the seldom-available Antitank Shell 40, 108 mm of armor plate [p. 84] cpuld be pierced. There were also several versions of the 7.5 cm 38/HL shell, the last of which, Typpe C, could pierce 100 mm of armor regardless of the range.

Production of the 7.5 cm tank destroyer cannon could be increased very quickly. While not even ten guns were delivered in March 1942, in August of that year the striven-for total of 150 was considerably exceeded, with 175 cannons delivered. Their immediate distribution to the troops brought new problems, the first of which was the lack of ammunition. The Chief of Army Equipping and Commander of the Replacement Army, Generaloberst Friedrich Fromm,

Penetrating power of the 7.5 cm Tank Destroyer Cannon 40, 7.5 cm Tank Destroyer Cannon 39 and 7.5 cm Assault Cannon 40 at an angle of 60 degrees and a plate firmness of 80-100 kg/mm³

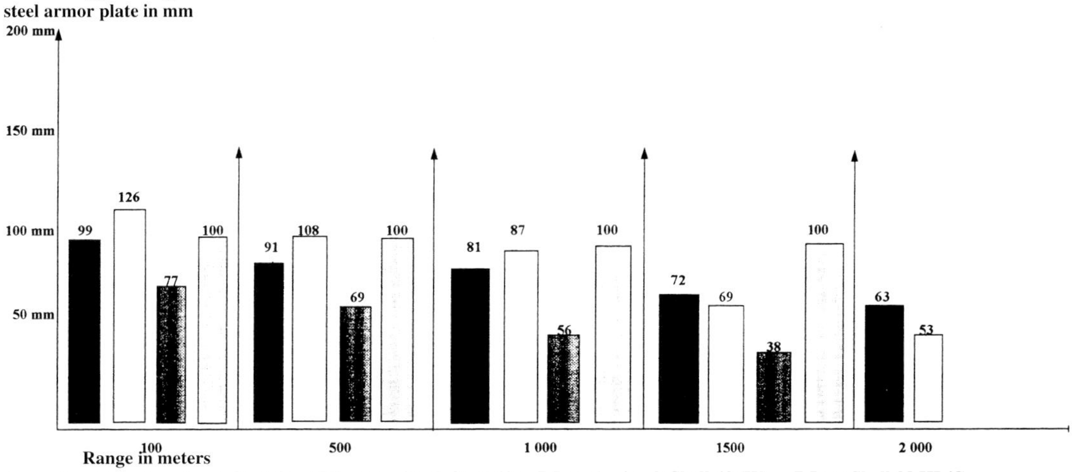

Legend: ■ 7.5 cm Antitank Shell 39 □ 7.5 cm Antitank Shell 40 ■ 7.5 cm Antitank Shell 40 (W) □ 7.5 cm Shell 38 HL/C

referred to this problem on May 1, 1942. For the heavy tank destroyer cannons promoted by the Army General Staff after the month of April, there was only one kind of ammunition available, and none at all for the 7.5 cm Tank Destroyer Cannon 41. This situation had to embitter the awaited delivery of the guns in May and June. A special problem under the code name of "Ullrich" was to help out; its goal was a considerable increase in the production of armor-piercing ammunition, The preparations for the realization of this program began with the involvement in July 1942 of the Rerich Minister for Armament and Ammunition, Fritz Todt. An easing of the tense ammunition situation took place only in 1943.

The second problem was a result of a considerable gain of weight by the new tank destroyer cannons. In place of the 980 kg, already regarded as too heavy, of the 5 cm Tank Destroyer Cannon 38, it was now 1190 to 1425 kg which had to be moved by motorized towing, along with the ammunition supply. Correspondingly powerful towing vehicles were lacking. The two models of light tractors, the 1-ton Demag D 7 (Sd.Kfz.10) and 3-ton Hanomag Hkl 6 (Sd.Kfz.11) were delivered in 1942 at 2868 and 1572 vehicles respectively. These numbers were not enough to be able to reequip the tank destroyer units for their rearming with heavy antitank guns, which began in

7,5 cm Pzgr Patr 39 Pak 40

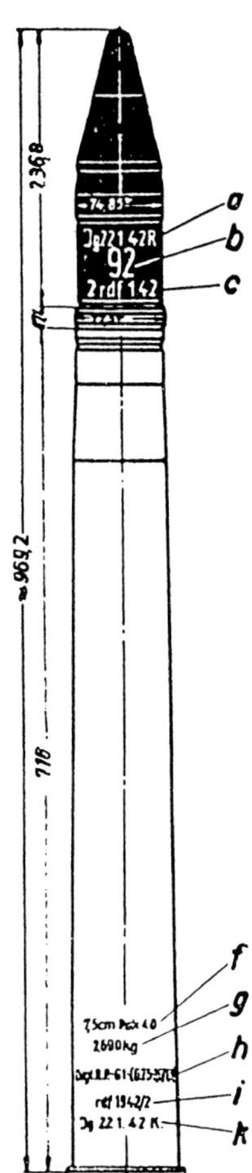

7,5 cm Pzgr Patr 40 Pak 40

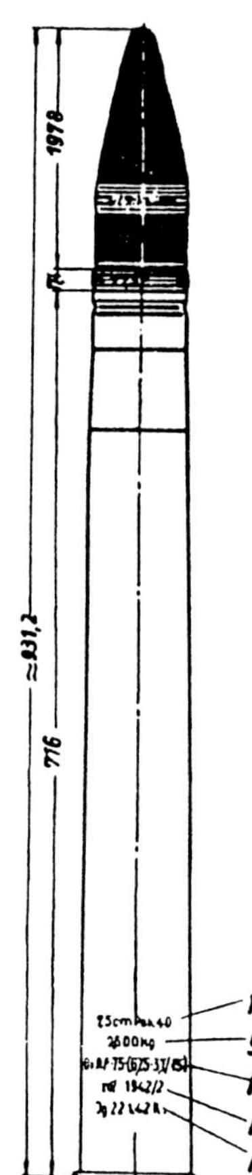

The standard gun of the German tank destroyer troops became the 7.5 cm Tank Destroyer Cannon 40. The production price was listed at 12,000 Reichsmark, the work required 2000 work hours. The life span of the barrel, 6000 rounds, was well above that of the 7.5 cm Tank Destroyer Cannon 41, which became the alternative model with a conical barrel.

the spring of 1942. Large numbers of makeshift towing vehicles were thus assigned to the Armu High Command in the east. The Armored Army High Command 2 received, along with 34 7.5 cm Tank Destroyer Cannon and 32 7.62 Tank Destroyer Cannon 36, 50 captured French Lorraine Tractors in May 1942. Assigning vehicles in hopes that guns would follow was not possible at that time. In the area of the 2nd Armored Army, other makeshift towing vehicles were used: Vickers-Armstrong and Lorraine tracked tractors, Somua halftracks. At the end of July they received 35 Renault armored ammunition carriers and 23 farm tractors. In some divisions medium off-road-capable (4x4) 3-ton Opel Blitz 3.6-6700 A trucks (17th Armored Division) or the not sufficiently strong one-ton light off-road (6x4) Krupp L 2H 143 trucks (Kfz. 69) (25th Infantry Division (mot), 56th Infantry Division, etc.) were used to tow the heavy guns. In a teletype on July 14, 1942 the High Command of Army Group Center stated that the horsedrawn 7.5 cm Tank Destroyer Cannon 97/38, lower in performance but then available in large numbers could be issued to the infantry tank destroyer companies of all troops. These were all makeshift measures, which also had to be used by the other army groups on the eastern front, but that, for very varied reasons, did not meet the needs of the tank destroyer troops. In particular, their mobility and off-road capability left something to be desired, and spare-parts supply became a problem.

One way to avoid needing towing tractors was to use self-propelled tank destroyer mounts. Practical experience with these vehicles was plentiful, even though the performance of the 4.7 cm Tank Destroyer Cannon (t) (Sfl) was no longer sufficient. In view of the great weight of the new heavy tank destroyer cannons, their installation on the light Panzer II and 38(t) tank chassis then available in large numbers seemed like a particularly good solution. Along with their off-road capability, comparable to that of the tanks, self-propelled tank destroyer mounts had a better readi

The weight of the 7.5 cm Tank Destroyer Cannonh 40 (1450 kg) caused serious problems for the Army troops. To be able to make the guns mobile, supply and artillery tractors from Belgium, France and Britain were issued to the troops. This picture shows such a unit (14th Armored Division) in the southern sector of the eastern front in the summer of 1942.

This 7.5 cm Tank Destroyer Cannon 40 is towed by a 3-ton (4x2) truck. The mobility of such a combination did not meet the expectations for the use of heavy antitank weapons.

Two-ton halftrack trucks of various types (Sd.Kfz.3) also appeared as towing vehicles for the 7.5 cm tank destroyer cannons.

When the 14th Armored Division was reestablished in France in March 1943, Tank Destroyer Unit 4 received new 5 and 7.5 cm tank destroyer cannons plus halftrack trucks as towing vehicles.

In 1940 the Belgian Army had used small Vickers-Armstrong towing tractors for the 568 kg SA-FRC heavy 4.7 cm Antitank Cannon. A few captured vehicles, designated Artillery Tractor VA 601 (b)—belg. Vickers-Armstrong—were used by the tank destroyer troops.

ness to fire and were protected by light armor from fire by infantry weapons and grenade splinters. On December 6, 1941, the Supreme Commander of the Army, Adolf Hitler, had already approved a suggestion of the General Army Office that 150 Panzer II flamethrowers be rebuilt into armored self-propelled mounts for heavy tank destroyer cannons (7.62 cm F.K.(r) or 7.5 cm Pak 44). The cited advantages were:

— Availability of an armored high-performance cannon,
— Saving of 150 towing vehicles,
— on the other hand, personnel and material shortages linked to the formation of flame-tank units were eliminated.

From this urging there came the Armored Self-propelled Mount I for 7.62 cm Tank Destroyer Cannon 36 (Sd.Kfz. 132). The development of a comparable tank destroyer on the dependable chassis of Tank 38(t) began with a request from the Inspection of Armored Troops on December 22, 1941. At the end of July 1942, according to a note in the war diary of Organizational Unit III in the Army General Staff on June 18, the first twenty 7.5 cm Tank Destroyer Cannon 40 on Lorraine Tractor(f) gun cars were expected. Troop testing by the 14th and 16th Armored Divisions (nine tank destroyers each) was planned. From then on, further examples of self-propelled tank destroyer mounts appeared. Here is a list of them:

In April 1942 the first armored Self-propelled Mount I for the 7.62 cm Tank Destroyer Cannon 36 (Sd.Kfz. 132) made by the Alkett and Wegmann firms were delivered. The 11.5-ton vehicles were created by rebuilding Panzer II flamethrowing tanks. They were used by the tank destroyer companies (Sfl) of armored divisions.

Vehicles of a tank destroyer unit, including armored Self-propelled Mount I, are loaded on a train. In war strength reports, Panzer I tanks (Sd.Kfz.111) with ammunition trailers (Sd.Anh.32/1) were foreseen as supply vehicles for tank destroyers.

Also in April 1942, the first Tank Destroyer 38 (t) for 7.62 Tank Destroyer Cannon 36 (Sd.Kfz.139) were delivered to tank destroyer units whose divisions were to see service in the southern sector of the eastern front.

Designation	Numbers and When Made
Self-propelled Mount 1 for 7.62 cm Tank Destroyer Cannon 36 on Panzerkampfwagen II D chassis (Sd.Kfz. 132)	201, April-June 1942
7.5 cm Tank Destroyer Cannon 40/2 on Panzerkampfwagen II chassis (Sfl) (Sd.Kfz. 131)	576, June 1942-June 1943 75, July 1943-March 1944
Tank Destroyer 38(t) for 7.62 cm Tank Destroyer Cannon 36 (Sd.Kfz. 139)	344, April-October 1942 19, 1943
7.5 cm Tank Destroyer Cannon 40/3 on Panzerkampfwagen 38(t), Type H (Sd.Kfz. 138)	242, November 1942-April 1943 175, 1943
Tank Destroyer 38(t) with 7.5 cm Tank Destroyer Cannon 40/3, Type M (Sd.Kfz. 138)	975, April 1943-May 1944
7.5 cm Tank Destroyer Cannon 40/1 on Gun Car Lorraine Tractor(f) (Sd.Kfz. 135)	170, July-August 1942
7.5 cm Tank Destroyer Cannon 40 on Gun Car FCM(f)	10, 1943
7.5 cm Tank Destroyer Cannon 40(Sfl) on Gun Car 39 H(f)	24, 1942
7.5 cm Tank Destroyer Cannon 40(Sfl) on Armored Tractor S 303(f)	1, 1944
7.62 cm Field Cannon 296(r) on Tank Destroyer Self-propelled Mount 5-ton Tractor	9, December 1941
Total	**2836**

The 7.5 cm Tank Destroyer Cannon 40/1 on the Lorraine Tractor gun car (f) bore the special vehicle number 135 (Sd.Kfz. 135) in the tank destroyer units.

The troops themselves created numerous provisional types to bridge the gap until the introduction of new antitank weapons and vehicles. This picture shows a 5 cm Tank Destroyer Cannon 38 on an armored Self-propelled Mount II.

At the end of 1942 the 7.5 cm Tank Destroyer Cannon 40/3 on the Panzer 38(t) chassis (Sd.Kfz. 138) was delivered as a tank destroyer vehicle.

A further, unknown number of self-propelled tank destroyer mounts came out of the troop workshops. In this context, a message from Army High Command on September 21, 1942 is of interest; it told of what means and by what work Panzer II tanks among the troops could be turned into self-propelled tank destroyer mounts. In one troop experiment there was a need for three NCO and ten men of the armored workshop platoon, plus radio personnel, who were able to carry out the rebuilding within two or three days. The example was supposed to set a pattern which, as was pointed out particularly, depended on the shipping of 7.5 cm tank destroyer cannons and other components, which could be expected only in the coming winter. Naturally, the self-propelled tank destroyer mounts that reached the troops in 1942 were in many ways only makeshift measures. The conception of a future [p. 93] fully armored tank destroyer depended very much on the armored Self-propelled Mount III for the 7.5 cm assault gun cannon, Type F/8, which was delivered to the assault gun units of the Army from February 1942 on.

The limited numbers of available medium and heavy tank destroyer cannons at first did not allow the uniform arming of infantry tank destroyer companies in the tank destroyer companies. For the year of 1942 there were the following equipping goals, based on the individual division types:

1. **In the Infantry Divisions**
   a. Infantry tank destroyer companies in regiments with two platoons with two 5 cm Tank Destroyer Cannon 38 each and two platoons with three 3.7 cm Tank Destroyer Cannon L/45 each.
   b. Tank destroyer companies in the tank destroyer units, each with one platoon of two 7.62 cm Tank Destroyer Cannon 36 and two platoons with four 3.7 cm Tank Destroyer Cannon L/45 each.

A 5 cm Tank Destroyer Cannon 38 on a 2-ton halftrack truck (Sd.Kfz. 3), with two Tank Destroyer 38(t) for 7.62 cm Tank Destroyer Cannon 36 (Sd.Kfz. 139) in the background.

Structure of an Infantry Tank Destroyer Company (of twelve guns)
(standing on the ground)
War Strength Report No. 186 F (notes) of December 1, 1942
(Type B[1])

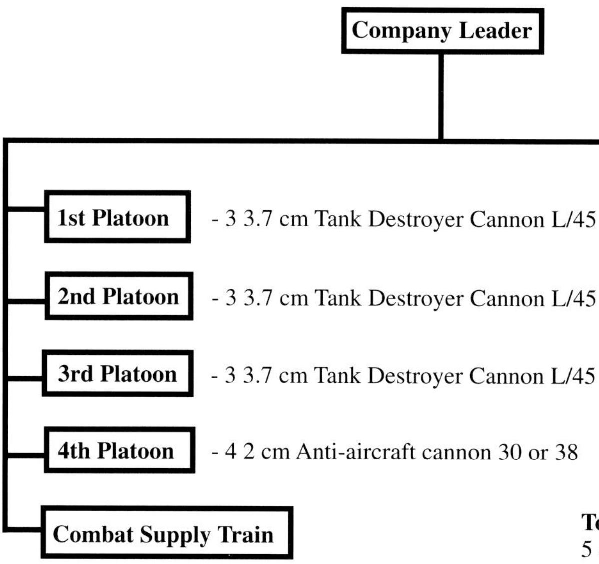

Total Strength
5 officers
29 NCO
96 men
9 3.7 cm Tank Destroyer Cannon L/45
4 2 cm AA Cannon
30 or 38

1. Composition A has four platoons with 3.7 cm Tank Destroyer Cannon L/45.

Special formations like SS police tank destroyer units were equipped with captured guns and vehicles. This picture shows the 4.5 cm Antitank Cannon 184/1(r)—russ. 37— towed by a truck likewise captured from the Russians.

The Russian Antitank Cannon 38, actually a 45 mm taznk gun in a makeshift box-spar mount, was seldom seen. A few examples of this gun type were used in the northern sector of the eastern front in 1943, designated 4.5 cm Antitank Cannon 184/6(r)—russ. 38—.

Firing training on the 4.5 cm Antitank Cannon 184/1(r)—russ. 37)—, which could effectively fight against 35 mm of armor plate at a range of 500 meters.

The Russian antitank cannons were not superior in fighting value to the comparable German gun, the 3.7 cm tank destroyer cannon. An advantage was the explosive shell, weighing over 2 kg, in fighting unarmored targets.

Penetrating power of foreign tank destroyer cannons in German service, at 500 meters, at an angle of 60 degrees and a plate firmness of 80-100 kg/mm

Penetrating power against steel armor plate (mm)

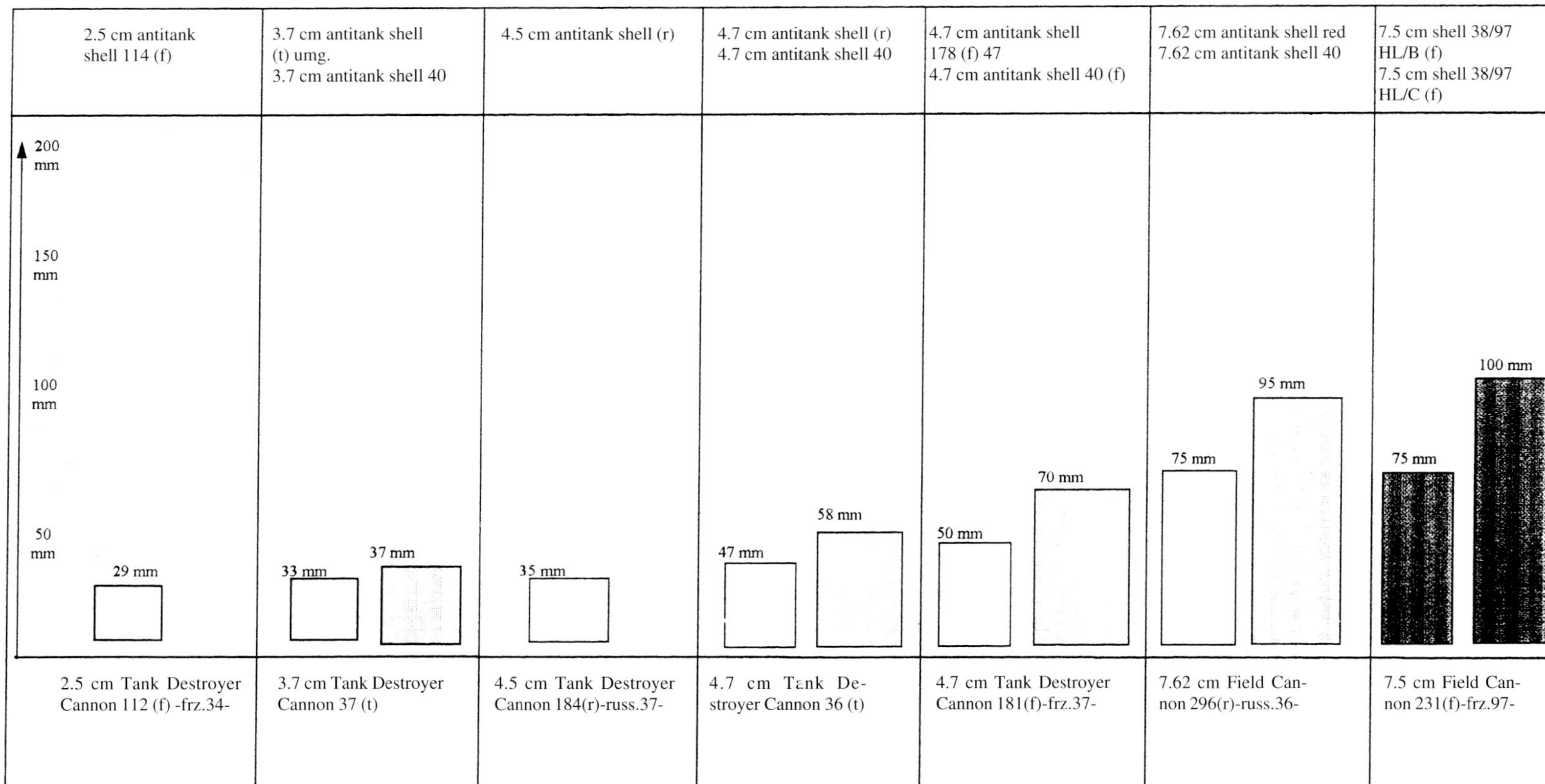

At the beginning of 1942, the Henschel and Rheinmetall-Borsig firms built two test models of the Armored Self-propelled Mount V. They were turned over to tank destroyer units in the east for front testing.

The chassis of the 35-ton Armored Self-propelled Mount V was made of components from the Henschel Panzer VK 3001. At first it fired 26.4-kilogram antitank shells (initial velocity 880 m/sec), which pierced an impressive 130 mm of armor plate at a range of 2000 meters.

By the end of 1941 the Magdeburg firm of Krupp-Gruson had delivered two Armored Self-propelled Mount IV a with 10.5 cm cannons. With the red antitank shell it penetrated 111 mm of armor plate at a range of 2000 meters. The self-propelled mount was tested on the eastern front in 1942.

1. The heavy Pak has proved itself fully. Even the heaviest armor of the KW.I and T-34 were pierced. Most successful are the heavy Pak on Sfl. and the 7.5 cm assault gun.
2. The use of the heavy Pak in the H.K.L. is to be avoided because most of them are ruined prematurely by fire from artillery or enemy tanks. The heavy Pak is to be used deep in the battlefield; it achieves the best effect through sudden strokes and flanking use. The letting-itself-be-rolled-over of the infantry has proved itself."

etration even of hull and turret fronts. A large number of the vehicles were burned out. Direct hits with the new 7.5 and 7.62 cm guns meant the destruction of the tank. At the end of the report, one can read: "The crews have agreed that they now feel superior to the heaviest Russian tanks in fighting value."

In a collection of experiences in battle against the Red Army tanks, the superior off-road capability of the T-34 tank was noted again. The main weakness of that type of tank, the crew's limited chance of observation, was useful for the surprise attacks of the antitank weapons. Since only a few Russian tanks had

In June 1942 the first 7.5 cm Tank Destroyer Cannon 40/2 on Panzer II chassis (Sd.Kfz. 131) were delivered. By March 1944, over 600 vehicles of this type had been built.

To this was added:

6. Action of assault guns or heavy Pak on Sfl. in counterattacks against enemies broken into with tanks as well as driving off enemy counterattacks with tanks increase success notably."

The judgment of the Division Commander of the 22nd Armored Division as to the self-propelled tank destroyer mount, on hand for just a short time, was also very positive. The successful advance of his division north of Arma Eli in May 1942 was ascribed to a significant degree to the presence of the new weapons. Of the six self-propelled 7.62 cm tank destroyer mounts on Panzer 38(t) chassis which Tank Destroyer Unit 140 of this division had, only one was lost while 24 Russian tanks were shot down. At a range of 1800 meters, the ammunition use was four Aititank Shell 39 per tank shot down. After the battle, tanks inspected on the battlefield showed problemless penradio sets, the commanders had to drive ahead in an attack to show the direction. When they were shot down, the tank unit generally became leaderless. Light, medium and heavy tank destroyer cannons were to be combined into so-called Pak-battle troops. A deep structure of antitank forces, in which tank destroyer cannons were to be placed toward the rear in carefully chosen and camouflaged positions, was to be striven for. The formation of mobile reserves from self-propelled tank destroyer mounts (if possible, a platoon of three guns) was seen as especially important. If need be, mixed Flak combat troops could be used. As another means of using all weapons in fighting against tanks, close-range antitank forces gained importance. Their tasks were the destruction of damaged tanks and self-defense.

The year of 1942 can be characterized as the year of changes in the development of tank destroyer

The armored Self-propelled Mount I for 7.62 cm Tank Destroyer Cannon 36 (Sd.Kfz. 132) is seen on the eastern front in the summer of 1942. The upper picture does not show, as often described, one of the few vehicles with the 7.62 cm Field Cannon 296(r)—russ.36—(with a small muzzle brake). The muzzle brakes on the barrels were retouched by the censors before the pictures were published.

The 7.5 cm Tank Destroyer Cannon 97/38 was temporary. The use of the venerable French 75 mm Field Cannon mle. 1897 for this gun limited its performance considerably in battle against tanks. Yet it remained with the troops to the end of the war, though in small numbers.

troops. Numeous new antitank guns, sometimes makeshift and yet very effective, made the scene in growing numbers. The modern antitank cannons, as Oberst Seither wrote in the "Wehrtechnische Monatshefte" in 1943, took on a "field-cannon character". While antitank defense had long been the task of a special troop of tank destroyers in the German Army, now the decisive significance of the tank weapon made it necessary to have all weapons ready for it. Corresponding to the material situations and tactical requirements, the structure and action principles were changed. In 1942 the effectiveness of antitank defense increased in the fight against the Red Army's tanks, which had grown in both quality and quantity.

The weight of the 7.5 cm Tank Destroyer Cannon 97/38 was listed as 1190 kg. The 6.8 kg antitank shell (p) was fired with an initial velocity of 570 m/sec. The use of this gun with the 7.5 cm 38/97 HL/C (f) shell (4.8 kg, 450 m/sec) was still effective to the end of the war.

Front view of a Tank Destroyer 38 (t) for 7.62 cm Tank Destroyer Cannon 36 (Sd.Kfz. 139). The gun, along with its four-man crew, could carry 30 shells for the gun and 1200 rounds of machine-gun ammunition. The 140 HP engine gave it a speed of 45 kph, comparable to the tanks.

VII. The Main Task of Antitank Defense

At the beginning of September 1942, the Organization Department of the Army General Staff was occupied with planning the expansion of the Army troops during the coming winter. They wanted to be ready for the battles of 1943. All applicable recommendations were influenced by the following considerations:

1. The greatest possible strengthening of the front with heavy weapons.
2. The main problem on the eastern front remained defense against enemy tank attacks. The General Staff was worried to see signs of strengthening of Russian armored troops after the German pattern.

From this is was concluded, among other things, that the mobile troops especially suited for effective defense against tank attacks, which were not tactically limited by war structure, should be strengthened in terms of their armament and numbers. This meant the assault gun and Army tank destroyer units. The material planning for the further buildup of the tank destroyer troops was already finished at this point. The next equipping goal, which was to be reached by the spring of 1943, was definitely the rearming of all tank destroyer units (36 guns) with heavy tank destroyer cannons. For the infantry tank destroyer units, arming one platoon with heavy guns (7.5 or 7.62 cm) was planned. This added up to the following needs:

1. Needed for the field and replacement armies
   a. For each tank destroyer unit, 36, and for each heavy platoon in the infantry tank destroyer companies two heavy tank destroyer cannon in the field army, = circa 8600
   b. For the replacement army = circa 750
   c. To replace the expected losses to April 1, 1943 (150 guns per month) = circa 1650
   total = circa 11,000

2. Numbers on hand on May 1, 1942 and predicted new production until March 1, 1943
   a. On hand as of May 1, 1942
   5 cm Tank Destroyer Cannon 38 = circa 2500
   7.5 cm Tank Destroyer Cannon 40 – circa 130

A 7.5 cm Tank Destroyer Cannon 40 L/46 in firing position on the eastern front in the spring of 1943.

The War Strength Report listing of a fast tank destroyer company (7.5 or 7.62 cm Pak) (Sfl), No. 1148 a of December 1, 1942, foresaw in Equipment B tank destroyer platoons with four self-propelled mounts.

7.5 cm Tank Destroyer Cannon 41 and 7.62 cm Tank Destroyer Cannon 36 (including self-propelled mounts)	= circa 850
total	**= circa 3500**

b. New production until April 1, 1943 (assuming the planned production will stay the same to March 1943)

5 cm Tank Destroyer Cannon 38 (300 monthly)	= circa 3300
7.5 cm Tank Destroyer Cannon 40 (100 monthly to September, then 130)	= circa 1280
total	**= circa 4600**

If one adds the existing guns and the coming new production, the result shows a shortage of 2900 medium and heavy tank destroyer cannons compared to the reported needs of the field and replacement armies. A considered increase in production of these guns (7500 instead of 4600 by March 31, 1943) was unrealistic. Independently of that, a large part comprised the low-performance 5 cm tank destroyer cannons. With the use of all available production facilities, it was possible to increase the number of 7.5 cm antitank cannons by 700 as of May 1943. Of these, 592 guns were on wheeled mounts. In 1944 an average of 1000 cannons per month could be delivered. So gradually they succeeded in replacing the light and medium tank destroyer cannons in the tank destroyer units. According to a guideline of April 4, 1943, arming the three companies in the tank destroyer units with six heavy and four light tank destroyer cannons was to be planned on. The heavy tank destroyer platoons in the armored grenadier battalions, as well as the staff companies, according to War Strength reports valid since early April 1943, also received heavy tank destroyer cannons (three guns per platoon). Light and mediun tank destroyer cannons were to be turned over to the infantry tank destroyer companies. The most important gun on a wheeled mount was now the 7.5 cm Tank Destroyer 40, and so it remained to the war's end. Accordingly, the number of 5 cm Tank Destroyer Cannon 40 was decreasing. Their effective range against heavily armored targets remained limited to 400 meters with hard-core ammunition (5 cm Antitank Shell 40) and was thus insufficient.

In 1943 the Army tank destroyers received another very effective gun: the 8.8 cm Tank Destroyer Cannon 43. Its development resulted from Hitler's order of June 1942. A cannon was wanted with a penetrating power of 160 mm of armor plate at 1000 meters. The firms of F. Krupp AG and Rheinmetall GmbH took part in developing the various versions. As a transitional solution, the Army Weapons Office accepted a gun in which an 8.8 cm weapon with L/71 barrel length had been mounted in the mount of the 10 cm Light Cannon 41. The disadvantages of this design, weighing over 4.5 tons, was knowingly taken in the bargain for the sake of bringing the high-powered weapon into action on the front in the summer of 1943. For bringing an end to the developmental work on the promising Krupp design and starting it in series production in the first half of 1943 was no longer possible. The gun was delivered as of December 1943 with the designation of 8.8 cm Tank Destroyer Cannon 43. It featured a cross mount, which allowed the gun to be aimed without traversing limits. An advantage was the low overall profile (1.72 meters). Because of problems with production of the cross mount, only six guns were delivered in December 1943—and the next ones (139 of them) only in February 1944. Production of the 8.8 cm gun in Field Cannon Mount 41 was thus concluded in August 1944. The contract had called for 1400 guns. Meanwhile the gun was designated 8.8 cm Tank Destroyer Cannon 43/41.

In view of their penetrating power against armor plate, the two guns showed no differences in performance. With the 8.8 cm Antitank Shell 39-1, 185 mm were pierced at 500 meters, 165 mm at 1000 and 148 at 1500 meters. For the 8.8 cm Antitank Shell 40/43, these values were higher (219/197/170 mm). But they were seldom available. Noteworthy achievements! The price for them was the meager life span of the barrel: 1200 rounds per barrel with regular use of the Antitank Shell 39-1 (7.5 cm Tank Destroyer Cannon, 6000 rounds). In the H.Dv. 119/329-Temporary "Temporary Shot Tables . . ." of June 1943, this problem was particularly noted: "In regard to the life span

The 8.8 cm Tank Destroyer Cannon 43/41 (L/71) reached the Army's tank destroyer units in 1943. In H.Dv. 119/329 its weight in firing position is listed as 4400 kg. The barrel was 6280 mm long without a muzzle brake. The Tank Shell 39/1 had an initial velocity of 1000 m/sec.

The highest possible production of the 8.8 cm tank destroyer cannon was given a special status in 1943. But the gun in the field cannon mount, at least, failed to live up to the high expectations. The weapon was too heavy for the tank destroyers.

Like the 7.5 cm Tank Destroyer Cannon 40, the 8.8 cm gun lacked suitable towing vehicles. Makeshift means like the use of the truck shown here did not work out. For this reason, small weapons carriers for the well-performing weapons were developed.

Penetrating Power of the 8.8 cm Tank Destroyer Cannon 43, 43/1, 43/2, 43/3 and 43/41 at an angle of 60 degrees and a plate firmness of 80-100 kg/mm²

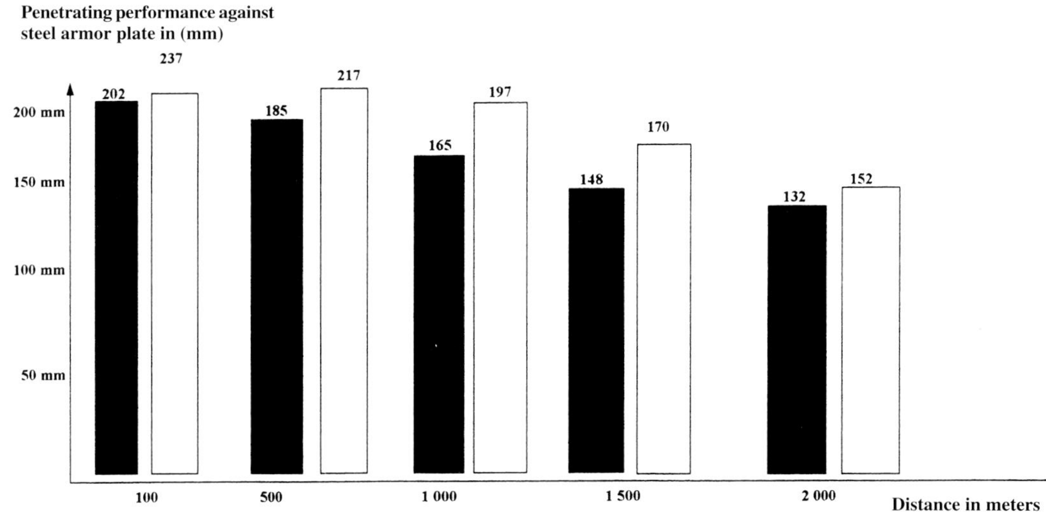

Legend: ■ 8.8 cm Antitank Shell 39-1 □ 8.8 cm Antitank Shell 40/43

of the barrels, the 8.8 cm Tank Shell 39-1 . . . 39/43 and . . . 40/43 may be fired only in absolutely necessary cases—against tanks."

In making the 8.8 cm Tank Destroyer Cannon 43 mobile in a wheeled mountd, similar problems to those of the earlier 7.5 cm gun arose, but they were especially serious because of the great weight. The firtst tank destroyer cannons of this type reached the troops in April 1943. A large number of the finished weapons were delivered for installation in self-propelled tank destroyer mounts. Besides the fact that there were efforts from the start [p. 109] to put the gun to use in the artillery (on May 16, 1943 the Jüterbog Artillery School was sent four of the guns), the 8.8 cm Tank Destroyer Cannon 43/41 and 43 was a weapon of the Army tank destroyer units. Until June 5, 1943 appropriate units of Army Groups South and A, as well as those of High Command West, received 173 guns, and 36 were ready for Army Groups Center and North. In all, 36 guns belonged to each unit. According to War Strength Report No. 1146 of May 15, 1943, their three companies (mot Z) were each divided into three platoons of four guns. The intended towing vehicles were 5-ton (Sd.Kfz. 6) or 8-ton towing trucks (Sd.Kfz. 7). The constant shortage of these valuable vehicles meant that in September 1943 the 4.5-ton "Maultier" tracked trucks, first delivered then, had to be assigned. The maneuverability of the Army

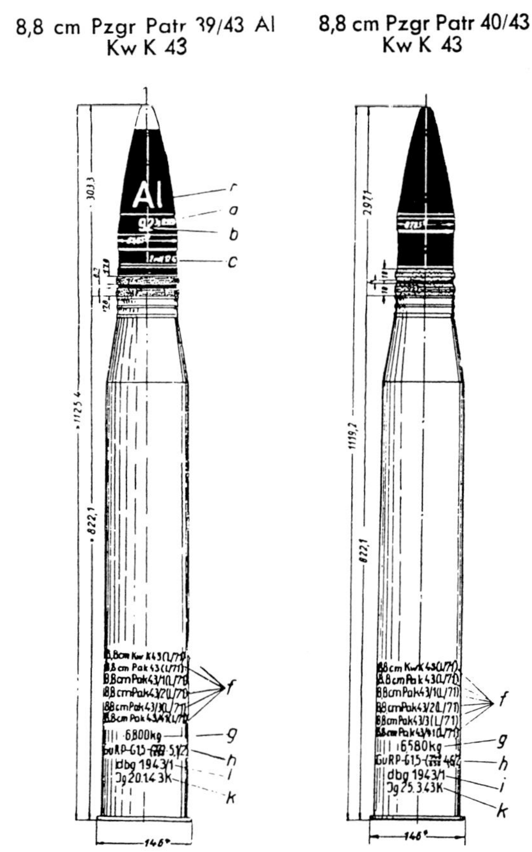

The Deutsche Eisenwerke began to deliver of the first 8.8 cm Tank Destroyer Cannon 43/1 (L/71) on Gun Car III/IV (Sd.Kfz. 164) in February 1943. 500 of them had been ordered, 494 were completed. The weight was listed as 24 tons; the armor offered protection from infantry weapons and splinters.

The 8.8 cm Tank Destroyer Cannon 43 (L/71) in firing position. The shield is missing (above). In firing position the gun weighed 3700 kg; in marching trim it weighed up to 5400 kg. Production ended in March 1945.

tank destroyer units to be moved by motor vehicles was thus limited. In an experience report from the eastern front in 1943 it is shown that a unit could be outmaneuvered by Russian tanks. It lost almost all its guns. In the "Nachrichtenblatt der Panzertruppe" of April 1944 the conclusion was drawn that the 8.8 cm Tank Destroyer Cannon 43/41. because of its weight and traversing difficulty, was not suited for mobile combat, and its use was practical only in "fixed places" or "fixed fronts". In the autumn of 1944 the Führer made a decision, according to which 7.5 and 8.8 cm tank destroyer cannons were to be used in great num bers by the Army and divisional artillery. Their own battle order thus received another antitank component, and the demands on the guns' maneuverability were not as high as in the tank destroyer troops.

Because of the expected high weight of the 8.8 cm tank destroyer cannon, its installation in a partly armored self-propelled tank destroyer mount was foreseen from the start. The Altmärkische Kettenfabrik firm of Borsigwalde had developed the Gun Car III/IV for it, and it was also used for the heavy howitzers of the armored artillery. In October 1942 a steel model of the self-propelled mount for the 8.8 cm Tank Destroyer Cannon 43/1 was displayed. Series production began in May 1943. The official designation was 8.8 cm Tank Destroyer Cannon 43/1 on Gun Car III/ IV(Sfl)(Sd.Kfz. 164) "Hornisse" (as of January 27, 1944 "Nashorn"). By March 1945 a total of 494 self-propelled mounts had been delivered. They saw service in Army tank destroyer units. One of the first was Army Tank Destroyer Unit 655, which was supplied with "Hornisse" in the summer of 1943. In the war structure of the field army as of mid-January 1944, five units were noted (No. 88, 93, 519, 560 and 655). Every unit had 45 self-propelled 8.8 cm tank destroyer mounts; there were 14 in the companies and three vehicles in the unit staff (tank destroyer equipment reserves).

Another tank destroyer vehicle with the 8.8 cm cannon, the "Ferdinand", first designated a heavy assault gun, was introduced in July 1943. The most spectacular action of the heavyweight Colossus was linked with the combat at the Kursk Bend. The decision to build a single series of such a vehicle was made on September 22, 1942, in order to make good use of available "Tiger" (P) tanks. The 8.8 cm Tank Destroyer Cannon 43/2 was installed. With mount and shield, it weighed 3.5 tons. Along with the heavy armor—200 mm on the front—the "Ferdinand" had a gross weight of 65 tons. 29 vehicles were delivered to the troops in April 1943, 56 in May, and the last four followed in June. Their planned use in the assault artillery did not take place. On the initiative of the newly appointed Inspector General of the Armored Troops, Generaloberst Heinz Guderian, two tank destroyer units were formed in March and April 1943. They were numbered 653 and 654. Each unit received 45 "Ferdinands", also called Tank Destroyer "Tiger" (P) (Sd.Kfz. 184). Both were included in Heavy Tank Destroyer Regiment 656 which was to have an important role during the attacks in the northern part of the Kursk Bend in July 1943. The tank destroyers of this regiment, with their heavy armament and armor, were to be put into situations where they could fight Russian tanks effectively at long ranges without themselves being exposed to the danger of being put out of action by tank-gun fire. The results after the heavy fighting did not look bad; with 19 total losses, the number of Russian tanks put out of action was given as 502—a result that could not make the problems of the "Ferdinand" assault guns disappear. They were restricted to attacks on armored targets at long ranges. Not even one machine gun for use against Russian close-combat antitank troops was on hand. Losses were not eliminated. One lot of the vehicles was stranded because of the mechanical sensitivity of the entire design and had to be blown up by their own crews. After further action in Russia and Italy, there were still 14 assault guns left at the end of 1944, now bearing the name of "Elefant". The last of them saw service with Heavy Tank Destroyer Company 614 south of Berlin in April 1945.

In 1942-43 more energetic efforts were obviously made in Germany to establish the 8.8 cm caliber guns, already successful in antitank action, in the tank destroyer troops. Yet the results were modest: In 1943, 780 8.8 cm tank destroyer cannons were delivered. They came in various mounts, quite in the spirit of the D 87 "Guidelines for Antitank Defense by All Weapons" of 1936, to see action in the tank destroyer troops of the corps and army groups. Their use had been foreseen only on orders from above and in front sectors particularly threatened by tank attacks. The equipment of the infantry regiments and divisions with 8.8 cm caliber antitank weapons was not planned. Guns with calibers up to 7.62 mm were reserved for them. In the spring and summer of 1943, their arming, as well as

In April and May 1943, a single series of 90 assault guns was built for the 8.8 cm Tank Destroyer Cannon 43/2 (Sd.Kfz. 184) and delivered. The weight was 65 tons, the heaviest armor was 200 mm thick.

The ninety giants known as Assault Tank Tiger (P), "Ferdinand" and finally "Elefant", saw service with Army Tank Destroyer Units 653 and 654.

In service, the "Ferdinand" suffered from numerous technical faults. During Operation "Zitadelle" at the Kursk Bend, 19 of them were lost, largely to direct artillery hits, while four caught fire from technical problems.

The effect of the 8.8 cm Tank Destroyer Cannon 43/2 (L/71) agaginst armored targets at long ranges was excellent, as shown by the many tanks shot down by army tank destroyer units in July 1943.

their equipping with towing vehicles and equipment, was determined in many cases by compromises and makeshift solutions. This applied less to the tank destroyer units in the divisions, which according to the aforementioned guidelines of April 1943 received one platoon of light and two platoons of heavy antitank guns (= four light and six heavy guns). The arming of the 14th Infantry tank destroyer companies in the infantry regiments was much more varied. In the addendum to a message from the Armored Army High Command 2 Ia/Id No. 1510/43 geh. of April 4, 1943, the following equipment was suggested:

a. Heavy tank destroyer cannons, 7.5 cm Tank Destroyer Cannon 97/38, two guns,
b. Medium tank destroyer cannons, 5 cm Tank Destroyer Cannon 38; 4.5 cm Tank Destroyer Cannon 184(r)—russ. 37, two to four guns,
c. Light tank destroyer cannons, 3.7 cm Tank Destroyer Cannon L/45, six guns

Independently of the fact that the number of delivered 7.5 cm Tank Destroyer Cannon 40 in 1943 was not enough to make a thorough arming of the infantry tank destroyers possible, this gun was simply too heavy for front-line use by the infantry. The same was true of the 5 cm Tank Destroyer Cannon 38. If one wanted to meet the expected demands of combat against tanks in the coming months, it was necessary to equip the infantry tank destroyers with high-performance new weapons. They formed the front line of a deep-structured antitank defense. Their weapons had to have a high likelihood of destruction (= high penetration) combined with simple handling, low weight and measurements as small as possible. Such divergent demands made the use of new devel-

The front surfaces of this "Ferdinand" have had 100 mm armor plates screwed onto their armor, which was made 200 mm thick.

One of the two Maybach HL-120 TRM engines with attached generator is being removed.

Field repair of a "Ferdinand" assault tank. On April 17, 1944 Heavy Tank Destroyer Unit 653 still had twelve vehicles of this type ready for action. Their name had meanwhile been changed to "Elefant".

The First Company of Army Tank Destroyer Unit 653 was transferred to Italy in February 1944 and saw action near Nettuno. This photo shows one of the vehicles captured by the Allies there.

Structure of a Heavy Tiger (P) Army Tank Destroyer Unit,
as of 1943

Unit Commander

- **Staff Company** with 3 Tiger (P) Tank Destroyers (Sd.Kfz. 184)
  6 Fla Sfl (Sd.Kfz. 7/1)
  3 2 cm Fla quads
- **1st Tank Destroyer Company** with 14 Tiger (P) Tank Destroyers (Sd.Kfz. 184)
  2 halftrack 2-ton trucks (Sd.Kfz. 3)
- **2nd Tank Destroyer Company** with 14 Tiger (p) Tank Destroyers (Sd.Kfz. 184)
  2 halftrack 2-ton trucks (Sd.Kfz. 3)
- **3rd Tank Destroyer Company** with 14 Tiger (P) Tank Destroyers
  2 halftrack 2-ton trucks (Sd.Kfz. 3)
- **Repair Shop Company**

Total Strength
45 Tiger (P) Tank Destroyers (Sd.Kfz. 184)
6 Fla Sfl (Sd.Kfz. 7/1)

opments in weapons technology, in this case rocket drive for shot movement, and the hollow-charge effect of shot results, urgently needed. The development initiated by the Army Weapons Office was advanced by a new weapon, which had appeared on the Allied side in the spring of 1943. In Tunisia several American 2.36-inch "Bazooka" rocket launchers were captured, and their evaluation brought important knowledge for German developmental work. According to a note in the war diary of Organization Department III of the Army General Staff on April 25, 1943, there were two weapons being developed at that time:

a. The 8.8 cm rocket launcher on a light mount,
b. The 8.8 cm rocket Panzerbüchse.

Tank Destroyer 38 (t) with 7.5 cm Tank Destroyer Cannon 40/3 (Sd.Kfz. 138)

Both reached the troops only in the late autumn of 1943 and influenced infantry tank defense in the last year of the war.

Let us look again at the armaments of the tank destroyer units. The most important and effective weapons in 1942-43 were the self-propelled tank destroyer mounts. Despite their good performance, experience clearly showed that they could be only a temporary solution. The tank destroyer troops needed fully armored light tank destroyers (= pursuit tanks) that were less vulnerable to enemy artillery and tank-gun fire. This recognition very soon resulted in tactical-technical requirements which were also a part of the theoretical discussions of the thirties.

In September 1942 the Army Weapons Office gave a development contract to the VOMAG firm of Plauen. The Panzer IV was to serve as the chassis for the light tank destroyer. Prototypes could be expected only at the end of 1943, and large numbers of tank destroyer vehicles for use in the tank destroyer units could not be available before the summer of 1944. With these activities, though, important qualitative standards were set for the further development of the Army's tank destroyer troops. As a transitional solution, the transfer of a large number of armored self-propelled mounts for the 7.5 cm Assault Gun, Type G (Sd/Kfz. 142/1) was planned. The conceptions of Generaloberst Heinz Guderian after his promotion to Inspector-General of the Armored Troops on February 28, 1943 can be evaluated in this sense. In the interest of uniting all available production capacities under the realm of the armored troops, he tried to include the transfer of the assault-gun units that formerly belonged to the artillery. Guderian was not able to accomplish that. On March 9, 1943 he gave a talk in Vinniza before Hitler, the Wehrmacht High Command and parts of the Army General Staff. His basic concepts of antitank defense are summed up under Point 6 of his speech:

"Antitank defense will become more and more the main task of the assault guns, since all other antitank weapons have too little effect on the new enemy tanks or are exposed to too great losses.

"All divisions on the main fronts therefore need a certain supply of this weapon, while the secondary fronts must make do with providing reserves of the assault guns for the higher command and at first supply the divisions with tank destroyers on self-propelled mounts. To save personnel and materials, a gradual blending of the assault gun and tank destroyer units must not be avoided.

"The new heavy assault guns would be used only on the main fronts and only for special tasks. They are first of all tank destroyers."

The only thing that Guderian accomplished was that from May on, 100 armored self-propelled mounts for the 7.5 cm Assault Gun, Type G (Sd.Kfz. 142/1) were assigned to the tank troops every month. They were used as transitional equipment in the tank units, by tank and armored grenadier divisions, as well as for the pursuit tank companies, originally called assault gun units, in the tank destroyer troops. On July 15, 1943 the Army High Command already set forth its future conceptions on the expansion and new structure of the tank destroyer troops (Army High Command, Gen.St.d.H./Org. Abt. Nr.I/2191/43 gKdos of July 15, 1943). It was stated therein: The Army High Command intends to bring the division tank destroyers, platoon by platoon, into the following structure when their equipment arrives:

— Staff and Intelligence Platoon,
— One tank destroyer company with twelve heavy Pak (mot Z),
— One company with 14 heavy Pak (Sfl) or assault guns,
— One company of twelve 2 cm or nine 3.7 cm AA guns.

The rearming of individual tank destroyer companies (mot Z) in the tank destroyer units began in the late summer of 1943. Among the first to be given an assault gun company of ten vehicles were the tank destroyer units of the 6th and 7th Infantry Divisions of the X. Army Corps. By order of September 10, 1943, unneeded guns and vehicles had to be turned over to other companies; personnel of one company each were then transferred to Germany and reequipped there.

At the beginning of October, the bands returned to their units as 2nd (assault gun) companies. The partial equipping of the tank destroyer units with assault guns enabled them to take up the fight against tanks with greater hopes of success, or to pursue tanks in mobile combat. They had firepower, mobility and armor protection comparable to those of the tanks. Their low silhouette was an advantage, and the low cost of building assault guns was an sdvantage to army equipping.

Among the first innovations in the tank destroyer units was the inclusion of a 3rd (anti-aircraft) company with 2 cm or 3.7 cm guns. They were subordinated to the unit only in terms of economy and supplying. The division commander ordered their action. In divisions with their own anti-aircraft unit, these companies were omitted. In their place was a third tank destroyer company. This often happened in armored divisions, so that up to 42 7.5 cm tank destroyer cannons were on hand, some as self-propelled tank destroyers. Some units had all self-propelled mounts or assault guns. The restructuring of the tank destroyer units described here brought further personnel and material expenses in terms of logistics. In the supply companies, the fuel and ammunition squads had to be strengthened. The same was true of the repair-shop squads. Their recovery groups received armored recovery tractors (Sd.Kfz. 136 or 164) only in 1944 instead of the 12-ton (Sd.Kfz. 8) and 18-ton heavy tractors (Sd.Kfz. 9). According to War Strength Report No. 1152 (free structure) of April 1, 1944, the supply company consisted of 192 men. For the fuel and ammunition squads there were a total of 21 3-ton and 4.5-ton trucks on hand. That made the tactical mobility of the tank destroyer units more difficult, and made their supply services a particularly important but very sensitive part. A problem for the ammunition supply was that the shells for the 7.5 cm tank destroyer cannon in wheeled or self-propelled mount did not fit the

An 8.8 cm Tank Destroyer Cannon 43/41 firing.

7.5 cm Assault Cannon 40. Despite their equal power, their shells had a different shape.

The restructuring of the tank destroyer units lasted until mid-1944; in some divisions it was never actually finished. The main reason must be seen in the rapidly increasing losses of weapons and equipment. In 1943 the new production of 7334 7.5 cm Tank Destroyer Cannon 40 on wheeled mount outbalanced their 2332 total losses. In 1944 10,937 cannons of this type came out of the factories, while the losses rose to 7579. From November 1943 to November of the next year, about 1000 7.5 cm and 241 8.8 cm self-propelled tank destroyer mounts were lost.

Structure of a Fast Tank Destroyer Unit in an Armored Division as of November 1943 (war budget)

Unit Commander

- **Staff Company** with 3 7.5 cm or 7.62 cm self-propelled tank destroyers (Sd.Kfz. 131, 132, 138 or 139)
  6 AA Sfl (Sd.Kfz. 7/1)
  3 2 cm AA quad
  3 12-ton tractors (Sd.Kfz. 8)
- **1st Fast Tank Destroyer Company** with 14 7.5 cm or 7.62 cm self-propelled tank destroyers (Sd.Kfz. 131, 132, 138 or 139)
  2 2-ton halftrack trucks (Sd.Kfz. 3)
- **2nd Dast Tank Destroyer Company** with 14 7.5 cm or 7.62 cm self-propelled tank destroyers (Sd.Kfz. 131, 132, 138 or 139)
  2 2-ton halftrack trucks (Sd.Kfz. 3)
- **3rd Fast Tank Destroyer Company** with 14 7.5 cm or 7.62 cm self-propelled tank destroyers (Sd.Kfz. 131, 132, 138 or 139)
  2 2-ton halftrack trucks (Sd.Kfz. 3)

Total Strength
45 7.5 cm or 7.62 cm self-propelled tank destroyers (Sd.Kfz. 131, 132, 138 or 139)
6 AA Sfl (Sd.Kfz. 7/1)
3 12-ton tractors (Sd.Kfz. 8)

Structure of a Staff Company of an Armored Grenadier Regiment
War Strength Report No. 1153 of November 1, 1943

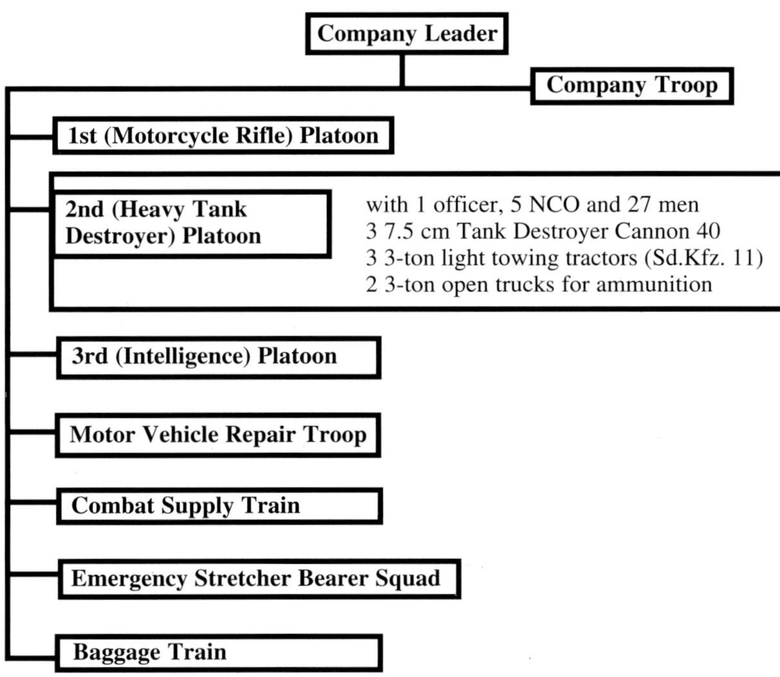

In 1944, as a rule, a company in a tank destroyer unit of the armored and armored grenadier divisions had 7.5 cm tank destroyer cannons (mot Z) with 1-ton light Demag D 7 tractors (Sd.Kfz. 10). In the tank destroyer units of the infantry divisions, the Tracked Tractor East (R.S.O.) was used instead.

The last version of the self-propelled mount on Light Tank 38 (t) chassis, Version M, reached the troops as of April 1943.

As transitional equipment, a few companies in the tank destroyer units of all division types were equipped with Assault Gun III (Sd.Kfz.142/1), Type G. The performance of the 7.5 cm Assault Cannon 40 was identical to that of the Tank Destroyer Cannon 40.

The wide traversing field of the 7.5 cm Tank Destroyer Cannon 40 is easy to see. This picture was taken in Tank Destroyer Unit 4 in the summer of 1944.

This picture from the eastern campaign was taken in 1944. The towing vehicle for the 7.5 cm tank destroyer cannon was a 3-ton Hl k 6 light tractor (Sd.Kfz, 11).

Loading a 7.5 cm Tank Destroyer Cannon 40. In the background is the Tracked Tractor East (R.S.O.) that towed it. With this vehicle, marching speeds up to 17 kph could be attained.

VIII. Achievements of the Tank Destroyer Troops

What is more appropriate than evaluating the performance ability of the tank destroyer troops by their shooting-down success? But there the problems begin. In general, the available figures for shot-down tanks are based on high estimates, which were based in turn on troop reports. Of these, depending on the time of year and the type of combat, between 20 and 50% have to be subtracxted for double reports and reparable tanks. The figures thus derived provide nearly exact data on the enemy's total losses in tanks.

It was even more complicated to link these figures with individual weapons. The defense against tank attacks had become the most important task of all forces and means. They had to include the infantry, the artillery including the assault guns, the armored troops with their tank destroyers, the engineers, even the backline services equally. Valid individual data on shooting-down success by the tank destroyer troops, which had to be recorded by the staff officers for antitank combat, are only fragmentary.

Let us look first at some individual examples:

1. **Army Group Loch (I. and XXXXIII. Army Corps, Eastern Front**

   In the report period (October 1-November 7, 1943) in the sector of the Loch Army Group, a total of 1000 Russian tanks and self-propelled guns were shot down On the basis of experience, a share of about 10% fell to the available means of close-combat an titank combat.

   The scores for the artillery and the German tanks can be ignored. In October 1943 there were only ten tanks (five of them captured) with the troops. Thus about 90% of the scores were made by the 391 tank destroyer cannons and 21 assault guns (three with 7.5 cm Assault Cannon 37 L/24). The crew of every fourth armor-piercing weapon could claim to have shot one tank down. The assortment of the 391 tank destroyer cannons in the Loch Army Group is very significant:

   10 8.8 cm Tank Destroyer Cannon 43/41
   121 7.5 cm Tank Destroyer Cannon 40
   39 7.5 cm Tank Destroyer Cannon 97/38
   84 5 cm Tank Destroyer Cannon 38
   137 3.7 cm Tank Destroyer Cannon L/45.

   The obsolete 3.7 cm and 5 cm guns still constituted far more than half the supply.

2. **Army High Command 19 (XIV. Armored Corps and LI. Mountain Corps), Italy**

   In May 1944, 432 tanks were reported shot down in the sector of the 10th Army. Of them, 205 (=47.5%) were scored by the 7.5 cm tank destroyer cannons, 93 by 7.5 cm and 8.8 cm self-propelled tank destroyers, and 118 by assault guns (53 of them by Italian vehicles). The other scores were attributed to the close-combat antitank means (11.5%), the artillery (15%), the tanks (13%) and other weapons (13%). The contribution of the self-propelled tank destroyers of the XIV. Armored and LI. Mountain Corps in the total is significant; their 72 tanks shot down rank well over the average. The assault-gun units could function less advantageously in the mouitainous terrain. In all, these statistics show again the superiority of the armored and self-propelled tank destroyer cannons.

3. **Army High Command 9 (CI. Army Corps, LVI. Armored Corps, XI. SS Armored Corps and V. SS Mountain Corps), Eastern Front**

   In the period from February 1 to 28, 1945, in the sector of the 9th Army, 79 Red Army tanks were shot down. Fewer than half, actually 31, were scored by the tank destroyers and assault guns (24 were shot down by assault guns, seven were put out of action by tank destroyer cannons). Ranking second were the close-combat antitank weapons (30 tanks shot down). followed by the artillery (15 tanks shot down). German tank crews could shoot down only three of their opponents. The high number of tanks shot down by assault guns and tank destroyers is striking. By then they dominated the weaponry in the tank destroyer units and assault gun brigades.

A precise report on the armored troops of the Red Army was submitted by the Army General Staff, Unit Foreign Armies East (IId), on October 10, 1944. It contains, listed by month and year, data on the Russian tank and assault gun losses from the beginning of the campaign in the east to August 1944.

Period	Tanks Lost
1941	22,000
1942	16,200
1943	18,850

1944 (through August)	13,740
Total	**70,790**

This number is nearly that of the Red Army's actual tank losses. These figures are based on the fact that figures on Russian tank production were also included in the report, and they show a remarkable agreement with the figures published after the war. It must be remembered how these figures were attained. They are based on the evaluation of factory numbers of shot-down tanks and self-propelled mounts. On the basis of the prevoisly evaluated individual examples from 1943, 1944 and 1945, it seems realistic to estimate the total number of tanks shot down by the tank destroyers in the report's time period as something between 25,000 and 30,000. This would equal the total year's production of 1944, in which the Soviet armaments industry produced 28,984 tanks and self-propelled mounts. The tank scores on the other fronts in North Africa, Italy and northwestern Europe are not included.

As for the correct evaluation of the growing numbers of tanks shot down on the eastern front between 1942 and 1944, they can be attributed only in part to the higher numbers and performance of the antitank weapons of the German forces. In 1942 the Army General Staff had already registered concern about the quantitative and qualitative strengthening of the Russian tank forces. This development had continued to grow. Until 1944 the leadership of the Red Army was still able to increase the numbers of their tank corps.

Nothing worked any more without tanks. Their increased use forced the loss figures upward without fulfilling the German hopes that the Russian offensives would come to a stop because of the high losses in men and materials. Here is a quote from the already cited report of the Department of Foreign Enemies East (IId) of October 10, 1944, in which the monthly production for July 1944 is listed at 2200 tanks and self-propelled mounts. It is further noted: "With this production plus tanks introduced from Great Britain and the USA, the Red Army's tank supplies could be raised to over 14,000 at the beginning of July 1943, and despite the steady high losses to the end of August 1944, could even be raised to over 18,000." The tank had become the decisive means of combat in land war. All German efforts to stop the flood of tanks in the east by stronger efforts in thec realm of armor-piercing weapons and ammunition remained unsuccessful. With that, at least since the summer of 1943, the outcome of the war was foreordained. Whoever knew the figures assembled by German reconnaissance could not be in doubt of that.

In January 1944, the name of the "Hornisse" tank destroyer was officially changed to "Nashorn". Early in April 1945 there were 141 of these vehicles on hand.

Captured Italian assault guns, with which a few companies in the tank destroyer units had been equipped, proved to be ineffective in battle. With the constant shortage of heavy weapons, though, they were a valuable reinforcement. This picture shows an M 43 *75/34) (I) Assault Gun—ital. Semoventi M 41 e M 43 da 75/34.

The 7.5 cm Tank Destroyer Cannon 40/3 in Tank Destroyer 38 (t), Version M, had a traversing range of 42 degrees and a ZF 3x8-degree targeting scope.

The vehicle also known as "Marder" III was very mobile (42 kph) and bore armor 8 to 20 mm thick.

In H. Dv. 473/5 b "Training Principles for the Armored Troops", Volume 5 b, "Training on the 7.5 cm Pak-Sf. 38" of December 7, 1943, self-propelled tank destroyers were described as follows: "Speed. off-road capability, . . . the great range of the weapon and the good sight conditions allow the Pak-Sf. to fight medium and heavy tanks."

IX. The Infantry Tank Destroyers in the Last War Year

In the Army they were determined to include an infantry tank destroyer company in every infantry regiment. Because of the tremendous importance of armored vehicles in combat conduct, it took on a special significance. It took over the protection of the forward parts of the regiment against tank attacks. The guns were brought into action from open but well-camouflaged firing positions. For light and medium tank destroyer cannons, that were still present in goodly numbers, flanking effects were sought as a manter of principle. Concealed positions offered additional possibilities of opening fire surprisingly. Heavy tank destroyer cannons were to be placed at the front, where the position and terrain allowed, in order to have an effect before the main battle line. In the realm of effective shot ranges, the use of the greatest possible rate of fire was urged (10 to 16 rounds per minute). Sharp attention was repeatedly afforded to the right and, above all, most economical use of ammunition. In principle, hollow-charge shells were to be fired from the 7.5 cm Tank Destroyer Cannon 40. A condition: Distance and target could not endanger the success. The functioning safety of the 7.5 cm 38/HL shell was lower at short ranges because of the greater force of impact. Tanks with frontal armor could not be fought, or only with difficulty. Advantages of the hollow-charge ammunition were seen in its lower powder consumption and barrel wear. The 7.5 cm Antitank Shell 39 could be used only when it seemed urgently needed. In 1944 the 7.5 cm Antitank Shell 40 was hardly used any more.

At the beginning of 1944, the restructuring and rearming of the infantry tank destroyer units begun during the previous year was still in progress. With the acceptance of the 1944 Infantry Division War Structure, a number of further changes were made in the spring of 1944. The newly established 712th Infantry Division was an example of this. The 14th (infantry tank destroyer) Company in each regiment formerly had six 5 cm Tank Destroyer Cannon 38 and three 7.5 cm Tank Destroyer Cannon 97/38. Now the first two platoons each received 18 8.8 cm Rocket Panzerbüchse 54 ("Stovepipe" or "Panzerschreck") and were called tank destroyer platoons. War Strength Report No. 154 b came out on February 1, 1944 and included them. The third platoon received three 7.5 cm Tank Destroyer Cannon 97/38, and the fourth was also newly equipped, with three 7,5 cm Tank Destroyer Cannon 40. This effective gun was too heavy (1425 kg) for use in the infantry tank destroyer companies.

The really noteworthy innovations in the infantry tank destroyer companies of the infantry divisions in 1944 were the two tank destroyer platoons. With the Rocket Panzerbüchse they now had a new, light and very effective antitank weapon. It reached the troops in notable numbers as of the autumn of 1943 and was first found in the tank destroyer battalions. The shell of the Rocket Panzerbüchse, a hollow-charge shell, could pierce 160 mm of armor. Only the

A new, effective antitank weapon that reached the troops in 1943 was the 8.8 cm Rocket Panzerbüchse 54 or "Panzerschreck".

The 7.5 cm Tank Destroyer Cannon 97/38 with Tractor East (R.S.O.). The gun was supplied to the infantry tank destroyer companies in 1944.

The 8.8 cm Rocket Panzerbüchse 54 "Panzerschreck" was in series production by six firms in 1944. With a shield, the weapon weighed 11 kg, the shell 3.25 kg. Up to 160 mm of armor plate could be pierced by it. The production cost was listed as 70 Reichsmark, and it took ten work hours to build.

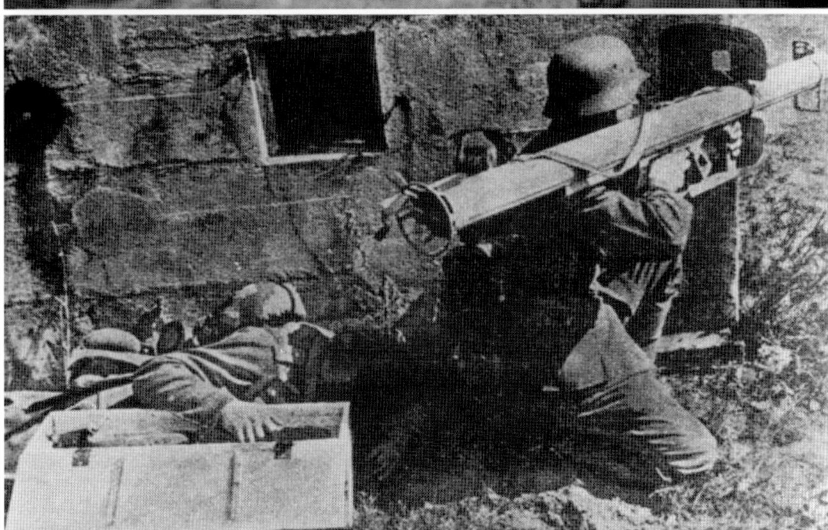

Another light antitank weapon for the infantry was the 8.8 cm Rocket Launcher 43. With a weight of 100 kg (in firing position), its power was not greater than that of the Rocket Panzerbüchse. Becamse of the much higher consumption of raw materials (200 kg of iron instead of 14.7 kg), its production was soon halted.

Structure of a Tank Destroyer Battalion as of 1944

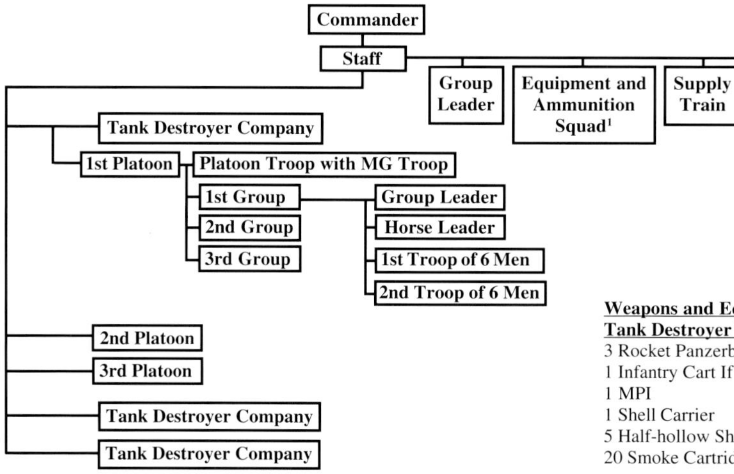

Weapons and Equipment of a Tank Destroyer Troop
3 Rocket Panzerbüchsen + 30 shells
1 Infantry Cart If 8
1 MPI
1 Shell Carrier
5 Half-hollow Shells or Panzerfäuste
20 Smoke Cartridges

1. An equipment or ammunition reserve of 54 Rocket Panzerbüchsen with 540 shells was carried by the equipment and ammunition squad.

range (150 meters) could stand improvement. In temperatures under -40 C it could be used only at ranges under 75 meters on account of the too-great scattering.

In weapon and ammunition production there were delays at first, thus the numbers of Rocket Panzerbüchsen increased significantly only in October 1944. 7800 of them were received. In May 1944 there were already 33,700 on hand, and the supply rose to 233,814 weapons of this type.

In October 1943 the establishment of tank destroyer battalions of three companies with 162 8.8 cm Rocket Panzerbüchsen was ordered. They also belonged to the infantry, but were listed as Army troops in the field army's war structure. As of February 1, 1944 there were nine tank destroyer battalions and five independent companies listed, but what with personnel shortages, they could not be completed in every case. They saw service exclusively with the army groups on the eastern front; two battalions with Army Group North were given a mixed supply of Rocket Panzerbüchsen and tank destroyer cannons. One can read of their use in "Guidelines for the Use of Tank Destroyer Battalions": "Tank Destroyer Battalions are antitank reserves of the high command, which presumably will be subordinated to the divisions for focal-point strengthening of antitank defense. . ." Their task was thus seen as the reinforcement of antitank defense in the eastern army at ranges up to 100 meters, a questionable decision because of the meager depth effect of this weapon. The use of the 8.8 cm Rocket Panzerbüchse 54 in the two tank destroyer platoons of the infantry tank destroyer companies, on the other hand, formed a sensible complement to the six tank destroyer cannons in the other two platoons. In Illustrated Pamphlet 149a "Close Combat Antitank Weapons, Part 1, Panzerschreck" of September 14, 1944 it was stated: "The Panzerschreck, because of its low weight and its simple handling, serves the antitank defense in the front lines. Its crew consists of the aiming gunner and the loading gunner. A tank destroyer troop consists of three "Panzerschreck" and forms the smallest combat unit. If possible, the tank destroyer group should consist of two troops in action together. In the composition of a "Panzerschreck" nest, according to side and depth, the effective ranges of the individual weapons should overlap. The nests must always allow all-around fire." The experience reports on the use of the 8.8 cm Rocket Panzerbüchse 54 were favorable, even though there were problems at first because of the lack of a shield and with the rocket ammunition. Rocket Panzerbüchsen and tank destroyer cannons could be used according to the terrain and complement each other's firepower. In depth and width, the effect of the Rocket Panzerbüchse troop was limited to 300-350 meters. Without support from other antitank weapons, they could quickly be outmaneuvered by tanks.

Parallel to the 8.8 cm Rocket Panzerbüchse 54, the 8.8 cm Rocket Launcher 43 was developed and put into series production in 1943. This weapon resembled a small gun and thus recalled the repeated efforts to create an infantry tank destroyer cannon to replace the obsolete 3.7 cm gun. Its weight in firing position was 100 kg. By comparison, the 8.8 cm Rocket Panzerbüchse 54 weighed 9.25 kg with comparable firing and penetrating power. The first 8.8 cm rocket launcher was delivered in November 1943; there were 732 of them in all. In February 1944 production had been halted. The numbers added up to 4301 in that month. This weapon was used on the same basis as the Rocket Panzerbüchse.

Rocket Panzerbüchsen were also used in the 14th (infantry tank destroyer) companies of the ground infantry divisions, which were restructured at the end of May 1944. It turned out to be disadvantageous that only the heavy platoon could be moved by motor vehicles. The medium and both tank destroyer platoons were horsedrawn. Extra light and medium guns remained as ground-standing armaments in the defense sectors. Thus they were robbed of a most important element for fighting against tanks, their mobility.

In the infantry divisions restructured according to a 1945 War Strength Report, the 14th (infantry tank destroyer) companies were all rearmed as tank destroyer units with 54 8.8 cm Rocket Panzerbüchsen 54 (plus 18 in reserve). In the tactical establishment of tank destroyer groups too, the depth effect of antitank weapons in the infantry regiments remained too meager, with a maximum range of 350 meters. The uniform arming with Rocket Panzerbüchsen remained a result of necessity. Thus the time until the introduction of the 8 cm Panzerwurfkanone 8 H 63 (PAW 600) was to be spanned.

In the German Army's infantry regiments, a strict division had been made in their artillery: There were infantry guns for use against unarmored targets, and their were antitank weapons for use against armored targets. This separation was maintained in the war, although with the increased calibers of the tank destroyer cannons, explosive shells with an effect comparable to that of the light infantry-gun shells were available. But tank destroyer cannons showed disadvantages in the variable forms of their trajectories, and besides, they were too heavy. All the same, the use of various guns in a regiment was more and more controversial. This burdened the limited production facilities for weapons and ammunition, made supplying the regiment difficult, and required additional personnel. Efforts to replace the infantry guns with grenade launchers were unsuccessful, although there

With the introduction of the 8 cm Antitank Launcher 600 (8 cm Panzerwurf Cannon 8 H 63), hopes grew for a final solution to the problem of antitank fighting by the infantry. The Launcher Hollow-charge Shell 4462 could pierce 140 mm of armor plate.

were attempts to fire hollow-charge ammunition (Wurfgranate 4462) from grenade launchers. For firing in the lower-angle realm, a gun was needed that could take on the tasks of the infantry and antitank guns alike. Here the 8.8 cm Panzerwerfer 600 offered a new solution in a weapon-technical sense. The firm of Rheinmetall GmbH had developed the gun. It could fire 2.75 kg fin-stabilized hollow-charge Launcher Grenades 4462 with a penetrating power of 140 mm of armor plate. The effective shot range against tanks was listed as 750 meters; otherwise 6200 meters were possible. The new high-low-pressure principle allowed a special barrel design, so that the cannon weighed 600 kg, more than half lighter than the 7.5 cm Tank Destroyer Cannon 40.

In January 1945 the troops received the first 81 launcher cannons, almost all from the Wolf firm in Magdeburg. On March 1, 1945 there were 155 guns of that type, and 34,800 rounds of ammunition were delivered. According to the War Strength Report No. 1141 of January 1, 1945, antitak companies (PAW) were to be set up with twelve 8.8 cm Panzerwurf Cannon 8 H 63. The saving of personnel was considerable, if one compares the 104 men of this unit with the 300-plus men who were needed for an infantry gun and an infantry tank destroyer company. But neither the new Panzerwurf Cannon nor the new structure brought a truly tangible strengthening of antitank defense. The number of new guns at hand was much too small for that; they were still found to some extent in troop testing. In April 1945 the Americans occupied the factory and thus brought an end to all further planning by the Army. The armament necessity program of January 1945 called for a monthly production of 1000 Panzerwurf Cannons, 4000,000 rounds of antitank shells and 800,000 rounds of explosive shells.

Let us turn our attention to another important subject, close antitank combat. According to the principles prevailing in the German Army at the begin-

In 1944-45 the 8.8 cm Rocket Launcher 43 (also called "Puppchen") was used by some units of the German Volkssturm. The 2.5 kg shells reached an initial velocity of 150 m/sec and pierced 150 to 160 mm of armor plate.

ning of World War II, it had been characterized as a means of "urgently necessary defense against tanks". In the war the German Army changed its mind about that. At the end of December 1943, the Chief of the Army General Staff, General of the Infantry Kurt Zeitzler, sent a message to the army groups and the Army High Command. In it he stated: "Close antitank combat takes on more and more meaning. Noteworthy success has been attained wherever all sol-

The Panzerfaust 30 m large (original shell called 30 m large) reached the troops in 1943.

diers of all branches were trained in close antitank combat." Close antitank combat was one form of combat that jumped over the boundaries between the different weapon areas. The infantry had to carry the main burden here, which is why the subject is also treated in the infantry tank destroyer section.

In the weapon and ammunition planning for 1944, the reduction of close-combat antitank weapons from thirteen different types to two was suggested. A development that was remarkable in every sense was that of the fist shell, which gained a certain fame as the "Panzerfaust". The developmental firm was the huge Schneider AG of Leipzig (HASAG). This piece of ammunition, steadily improved in its functioning safety and practical qualities, allowed the last version made, the "Panzerfaust" 100 m, to fight armored vehicles at ranges up to 300 meters (trajectory hight point 3.50 meters). The armor-penetrating power of the hollow-charge warhead was 200 mm of steel plate. In 1944 a total of 5,662,000 of the Panzerfaust were made. Further developments, like the "Panzerfaust" 150 m and the "Splitterfaust", were bring troop-tested at the end of the war; the "Panzerfaust" 250 m development was completed in the USA and USSR.

In the last months of the war, the "Panzerfaust" took on a great importance as the means of antitank combat. Tank destroyer and assault gun units received them in place of their specified armaments. They were the "poor man's antitank defense"! In the "Handbook for Close-combat Antitank Training" of October 28, 1944 one can read: "The focal point is the training of the single combatant with the Faust shell. Win as much of the tank's flank as possible with hunter-like stalking and let tanks approach." Deceptive in terms of opinion-building in the homeland war zone were

In the German Army the Panzerfaust was the most important means of close antitank combat. Up to 200 mm of armor could be pierced by the hollow-charge warhead.

newspaper reports, like this one from the Dresden morning paper, "Der Freiheitskampf" of October 27, 1944: "When within 48 hours just in the Goldap-Gumbinnen area 323 Soviet tanks can be destroyed, then this truly unusual defensive success may be attributed in large measure to the fact that theoretically, every infantryman with a Panzerfaust in his hand replaces a Pak gun."

According to a report from Army High Command 9 to the Inspector-General of the Armored Troops on March 10, 1945, in the Army's sector in February 1945, 30 of a total of 79 tank scores were achieved with close-combat weapons and methods (27 with the "Panzerfaust", three with the "Panzerschreck"). This was considerable success, indicating that attacking the tank-defense problem with close-combat means alone was false. The establishment of several hundred tank-defense commands in Army Groups Center and Vistula, carried on emphatically since the latter half of January, emphasizes how much hope contemporary success with close-combat antitank weapons had inspired. On April 20, 1945, War Strength Report No. 1148 (Makeshift) for bicycle-mobile antitank companies of the Army was issued. Commands consisting of one officer, one NCO and eight antitank close combatants, armed with assault guns and "Panzerfaust", attacked tanks on bicycles. They were the low point in the development of antitank defense in the German Army, at a time when the overwhelming role of the tank in warfare required a balanced system of antitank defense based on the cooperation of individual weapon types.

Tank destroyer companies had eighteen of the 8.8 cm Rocket Panzerbüchse 54. In 1944, individual companies of tank destroyer units in the divisions were equipped with them. In 1945 there was a thoroughgoing supplying of these weapons.

Again and again the troops tried to make up for the lack of self-propelled heavy antitank weapons by improvising. These pictures show a 7.5 cm Tank destroyer Cannon 97/38 on the chassis of a 738 (r)—russ. T-26—light tank.

X. The Development of Division Tank Destroyer Units in the Last War Year

The restructuring and rearming of the divisions' tank destroyer units undertaken in the summer of 1943 had not yet been completed until May 1944. Often the assault gun companies (referred to as assault gun units) were lacking, and often the anti-aircraft companies as well, so that a whole group of units had only one tank destroyer company (mot Z) with twelve guns. Naturally, rearming with the more capable 7.5 cm caliber formed a valuable strengthening of antitank defense. In May 1944, 470 7.5 cm Tank Destroyer Cannon 40 had been delivered; monthly production sank to 207 by December and even to 123 by March 1945. In comparison, the losses in those months numbered 507, 414 and 756 guns (February 1945). A downhill tendency was not ruled out by these figures.

Besides these guns, there were still decreasing numbers of the 7.5 cm Tank Destroyer Cannon 41 (11 in November 1944), 7.5 cm Tank Destroyer Cannon 97/38 (190 in November 1944, including 7.5 cm Field Cannon 231(f)), and 7.62 cm caliber weapons on wheeled mounts, with 81 still in the tank destroyer units. Their production was halted; the existing guns were used up.

An interesting troop experiment was begun by the 2nd Army (Army Group Center) in January 1944. On January 14 of that year, 60 7.5 cm Tank Destroyer Cannon 40/4 (Sfl) on Tractor East (R.S.O.) were assigned to it (radio message no. 15942 of January 14, 1944). They were divided as follows:

14 to Army Tank Destroyer Unit 744,
14 to Army Tank Destroyer Unit 743,
14 to the 18th Armored Grenadier Division,
8 to Ski Hunter Brigade 1,
10 as reserve equipment.

At the end of January 1944 there came an attempt by Army Group South. Efforts to load various guns, including tank destroyer cannons, onto the Tractor East (R.S.O.) for transport had already taken place in the summer of 1943. The reason was the effort to protect the weapons from going out of adjustment, which

Coastal defense along the Atlantic coast of northwestern France: The 7/5 cm Tank Destroyer Cannon 97/38 could be used as both an antitank gun and a light field gun. Its maximum range was listed as 11,000 meters with Explosive Shell 233/1(f).

A 7;5 cm Tank Destroyer Cannon 40/4 on Tractor East (R.S.O.). The front of the vehicle was lightly armored to protect the engine compartment.

often happened because of the rear steering motions of the fully tracked tractor. The Tractor East (R.S.O.) had meanwhile become one of the most important towing vehicles. Now this idea had resulted in a light, partly armored self-propelled mount. It was shown to Hitler as early as the autumn of 1943. He approved the project. The production of up to 400 tractors per month was planned. No figures survive to show how many were actually built.

The ski hunter brigade being established as 1943 changed to 1944 received seven, not the planned eight, 7.5 cm Tank Destroyer Cannon 40/4 on Tractor East (R.S.O.). They were used by two platoons of the tank destroyer anti-aircraft company of the brigade's heavy battalion. This company was structurally unique. Its slow speed (17.2 kph) compared to the tanks proved to be a disadvantage in action. The noise of the high-speed Steyr V-8 engine was too loud. Action in which the partly armored self-propelled mounts were used as assault guns for lack of other heavy weapons led to losses.

The war structure of the tank destroyer units in the armored and armored grenadier divisions agreed to a large extent. In the infantry divisions there were various structures and equippings:

Tank-destroyer men giving instructions, as seen on the eastern front in the spring of 1944.

Tank Destroyer Unit in	1st Company	2nd Company	3rd Company
Armored or Armored Grenadier Division Destroyer KSTN 1944	14 Assault Guns (Jagdpanzer)	14 Assault Guns (Jagdpanzer)	12 7.5 cm Tank Cannon (mot Z)
Infantry Division (KSTN 1944) 1st Structure Type	12 7.5 cm Tank Destroyer Cannon (mot Z)		
2nd Structure Type	12 or 9 7.5 cm Tank Destroyer Cannon (mot Z)	10 Assault Guns (Jagdpanzer)	a. 12 2 cm Flak Sfl. (or mot Z) b. 9 3.7 cm Flak (mot Z) c. 12 2 cm Mtn. Flak (mot Z)
3rd Structure Type	14 7.5 or 7.62 cm Pak (Sfl)	10 Assault Guns (Jagdpanzer)	as 2nd Structure Type
4th Structure Type	14 7.5 or 7.62 cm Pak (Sfl)	14 7.5 ot 7.62 cm (Sfl)	as 2nd Structure Type
5th Structure Type	10 Jagdpanzer and	10 Jagdpanzer and	as 2nd Structure Type
Armored Division KSTN 1945	Grenadier escort	Grenadier escort	Infantry Division as in KSTN 1944
Infantry Division KSTN 1945	12 7.5 cm Tank Destroyer Cannon (mot Z)	14 Assault Guns and Grenadier escort	9 3.7 cm Flak (mot Z)

A few 7.5 cm Tank Destroyer Cannon 40 were installed on chassis of captured French Hotchkiss H 39 cavalry tanks. They were used in the same manner as the self-propelled tank destroyer mounts on Panzer II and 38(t) chassis.

For the units of the 9th Wave, first called "barrage divisions" later grenadier divisions, which were established in great haste from July 1944 on, there was only an assault gun company. According to the War Strength Report of April 1, 1944, it was to have ten assault guns. The 3.7 cm anti-aircraft company of nine guns did not belong to the tank destroyer units of these divisions.

In practice there were considerable deviations from the war structure and specified equipping. Here are three examples: The 278th Infantry Division in Italy had been assigned Italian assault guns for its 2nd (assault gun) Company/Tank Destroyer Unit 278 in March 1944. They were all lost during the combat around San Biagio early in July 1944. It was the same on the eastern front. In September 1944, Tank Destroyer Unit 1542 of the 542nd Infantry Division had been established. Its 1st Company received, as temporary equipment, six 7.5 cm Tank Destroyer Cannon 40. They were towed by the Tractor East (R.S.O.), and the unit's supply trains were horsedrawn. The 2nd Company had, in addition to the specified assault guns, two Fla-Panzer 38(t) (2 cm). In October 1944the unit was able to shoot down 31 Russian tanks in three weeks at the Narev bridgehead, losing five assault guns and six tank destroyer cannons itself.

Tank Destroyer Unit 36 of the 36th People's Grenadier Division was in combat on the western front near Phillipsburg-Neunhofen in January 1945. In a situation report, the 2nd (assault gun) Company was particularly mentioned. It was supposed to have 14 vehicles; of the eleven assault guns on hand, eight were ready for action. Theirs crews had had brief training on the Jagdpanzer 38 (Sd.Kfz. 138/2) and now had to deal with the Assault Gun IV (Sd.Kfz. 167). This necessarily led to problems: "The replacements sent to us were not at all sufficiently trained. They were young drivers without experience, merely hav-

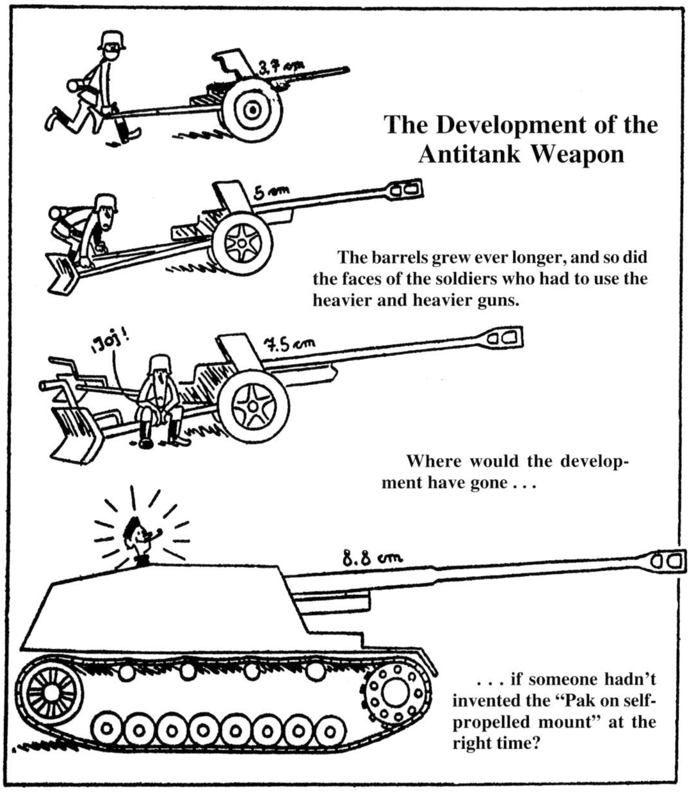

Contemporary caricature of the development of tank destroyer weapons (1944).

Structure of a Tank Destroyer Unit in an Armored Division, as of November 1944

- **Unit Commander**
  - **Staff Company** with 3 Jagdpanzer IV (Sd.Kfz. 162) or 38 (Sd.Kfz. 138/1)
    3 Fla Sfl (Sd.Kfz. 7/1)
  - **1st Tank Destroyer Company (mot Z)** with 12 7.5 cm Tank Destroyer Cannon 40 (mot Z)
    12 Light Machine Guns
  - **2nd Pursuit Tank Company** with 14 Jagdpanzer IV (Sd.Kfz. 162) or 38 (Sd.Kfz. 138/2)
    1 Halftrack Cycle (Sd.Kfz. 2)
    1 light personnel car
  - **3rd Pursuit Tank Company** with 14 Jagdpanzer IV (Sd.Kfz. 162) or 38 (Sd.Kfz. 138/2)
    1 Halftrack Cycle (Sd.Kfz. 2)
    1 light personnel car
  - **Supply Company** with 2 18-ton Towing Tractors (Sd.Kfz. 9)
    1 Recovery Tank IV (Sd.Kfz. 164)

Total Strength
31 Jagdpanzer (Sd.Kfz. 162 or 138/2)
12 7.5 cm Tank Destroyer Cannon 40
2 18-ton Towing Tractor (Sd.Kfz. 9)
1 Recovery Tank IV (Sd.Kfz. 164)

ing drivers' licences. . . ." As a result, some of the Maybach engines broke down before reaching their usual life span. The Tractor East (R.S.O.) used to tow the 7.5 cm Tank Destroyer Cannon 40 also drew criticism, namely: "The R.S.O. as towing vehicles for the mot-Z company are insufficient, since they constantly break down from technical problems. As an average, 60% of them are ready for action."

In the last year of the war, the use of tank destroyers in the front lines of the German defenses, formerly seen as advantageous, had been completely rejected. The impact of the tank attacks was too great for that. Thus they tried to situate the antitank weapons, and particularly those of the tank destroyer units, in the depths, so that the defenses could not be penetrated. Naturally the principle "The farther forward the antitank weapons fulfill their task, without themselves being shattered by enemy fire, the more losses they save the infantry and the better they protect the artillery positions," was still valid and worth

Self-propelled tank destroyer mounts were supposed to move on the enemy tanks through reciprocal fire support and clever terrain utilization, in order to let them move into favorable firing conditions and surprise them with sudden fire (H.Dz. 473/5 b).

According to War Budget 44, Pursuit Tank Company (Jagdpanzer IV or 38) No. 1149 (free structure), of November 1, 1944, the equipment of the three tank destroyer platoons with four pursuit tanks each was planned. One pursuit tank belonged to the group leader.

The Pursuit Tank 38 (Sd.Kfz. 138/2) was delivered as of April 1944 and ranked, along with the Pursuit Tank IV (Sd.Kfz. 162), among the most important vehicles in the pursuit tank companies of the tank destroyer units.

striving for. In practice, though, it could scarcely be done any more. Because of their sensitivity, tank destroyer cannons on wheel mounts were to be placed as far out of the enemy's main firing area as possible. What was more vital, was setting up a direct connection with the division artillery. In fact, there were numerous experiments in 1944. One concerned the establishment of infantry Pak units with three batteries of nine 7.5 cm Tank Destroyer Cannon 40 each, which was also called 7.5 cm Light Field Cannon 40 when taken over by the artillery. With the use of such units, which also belonged to the People's Artillery Corps, effective antitank defense was automatically concentrated at great depth in the German combat structure. The establishment of artillery Pak units suffered from personnel and material shortages (see Situation Report on Artillery Pak Unit 1061 of July 13, 1944).

As for the basic problems that arose with the use of tank destroyer cannons as light field cannons, this was also mentioned in an experience report on troop testing "Subordination of the Antitank Defenses to Artillery" of the Narva Army Unit in the summer of 1944. Listed as important weaknesses were:

1. Unified command was made difficult because of the varying nature of the weapons.
2. The barrel life span of heavy antitank guns was not sufficient. Their use in fulfilling artillery tasks influenced their targeting precision when firing on armored targets.
3. The protection of the infantry from tanks had to be limited to subordinating the antitank defenses to the artillery, and thus to the situation of the infantry tank destroyer companies deep in the German combat order.

The fact that the highest German military leadership nevertheless decided at the beginning of 1945 to transfer the 7.5 cm tank destroyer cannons on hand with the divisions to the artillery regiments as light field cannons was a result of tests in the summer of 1944 and the awareness bought with high losses and severe setbacks: Only the tank made the difference on the battlefield. To the extent that it would succeed in making antitank defense more successful, defense as a whole necessarily had to be made more

The sensitivity of the 7.5 cm Tank Destroyer Cannon 40 (mot Z) to artillery fire compelled the gun to be situated in the depths of the German combat order, where it could be used both as an antitank gun and also according to artillery principles as a light field cannon.

A 7.5 cm Tank Destroyer Cannon 40 damaged by artillery fire is seen in the armorer's yard of the staff company of a tank destroyer unit.

A 7.5 cm Tank Destroyer Cannon 40 waits in ambush. The surprising opening of fire in the area of favorable shot range was an important prerequisite for successful defense against tank attacks.

On January 14, 1945 the General Quartermaster Unit of the Army General Staff se nt word that the production of ammunition for the 7.5 cm Tank Destroyer Cannon 40 and 7.5 cm Light Field Cannon 7 M 85 were being cut by 62%.

resistant. For that, the artillery with their light cannons should do their job in the depths of the combat order. And that caused problems. Now the disadvantages of one-sided use of the 7.5 cm Tank Destroyer Cannon 40 as a high-performance gun for antitank defense became apparent. Its elevation and range were too meager, its power need for one shot too great, the manufacture of its shells was too complex and its barrel wear too great. The fulfilling of many firing tasks by the artillery depended on varying the shells' trajectories—which could not be done with this gun.

Basic decisions made after the beginning of January 1945 that concerned the divisions' tank destroyer units numbered only two, or three that dealt with all companies equipped with assault guns or pursuit tanks. In any case, they had proved to be the most effective means of antitank combat. How had the technical development in this area proceeded in the last war year? In 1943 the last tank destroyer on Panzer IV chassis, that had been ordered from Vomag in Plauen, had taken form. Above all, the shape and strength of the armor were much improved. On December 20, 1943 a soft steel prototype of the new type of vehicle, still described as a new type of assault gun, had been displayed. In January 1944 the first forty series vehicles had left the assembly halls of the works in Plauen. The official designation was Jagdpanzer IV (7.5 cm Pak 39 L/48) (Sd.Kfz. 162). The main waeapon installed was the 7.5 cm Tank Destroyer Cannon 39 L/48. The gun was mounted in a fairing, which helped to save weight and work in comparison with the installation of the 7.5 cm Assault Cannon 40 in the assault gun. Ammunition and penetrating power were the same. From the start it had been kept in mind that pursuit tanks should be similar in effect to assault guns, including against infantry. For that a machine gun, a machine pistol and a special close-combat weapon, that could be operated under armor protection, were planned.

The first Jagdpanzer IV went to the Tank Destroyer Training Unit in March 1944. They showed numerous faults and were evaluated as not ready for front use. Validity for personnel and material equipping came only with War Strength Report No. 1149 of Febauary 1, 1944, in which assault gun units (in tank destroyer units) of ten or fourteen guns were mentioned. On November 1, 1944 a different War Strength Report appeared with the same number. It served as War Budget 44 for a pursuit tank company (Jagdpanzer IV or 38)(free structure). An important difference besides the designation was that the personnel had been cut from 73 to 57 men with the same fighting value. Thus the personnel strength of the companies of the tank destroyer units had been decreased by less than one-third in comparison to 1941.

In 1942, with the completion of the development contract for the light tank destroyer, it was recognized that its armament with the 7.5 cm Tank Destroyer Cannon 39 could not keep pace indefinitely with further developments in tank construction. An available

A gunner aims a Pak with the ZF 38 3 x 8 aiming scope.

alternative was a 7.5 cm gun with L/70 barrel length. One specimen had been built in the autumn of 1942. It led to the 7.5 cm Tank Destroyer Cannon 42 L/70, the series production of which began in July 1944 at Skoda in Pilsen and the Gustloff works in Weimar. On April 20, 1944 a prototype of the Jagdpanzer IV with "over-long 7.5" had already been shown to Adolf Hitler, the Reich Chancellor and Supreme Commander of the German Wehrmacht. This type received the official designation of Panzer IV long (Vomag) (Sd.Kfz. 162/1). Hitler arranged to have

Front view of the Jagdpanzer IV pursuit tank (Sd.Kfz. 162), Type F. The first vehicles of this type were delivered in January 1944. The gun, the Tank Destroyer Cannon 39, was made for the same ammunition as the 7.5 cm Tank Gun and Assault Gun.

The 60 mm armor (80 mm fairing), the flat shape and the high mobility of the Jagdpanzer IV (Sd.Kfz. 162), Type F, allowed attacks to be made on tanks, meaning to pursue them according to the original concept of the tank destroyer troops.

Penetrating Performance of the 7.5 cm Tank Destroyer Cannon 42 at an angle of 60 degrees and a plate firmness of 80-100 kg/mm²

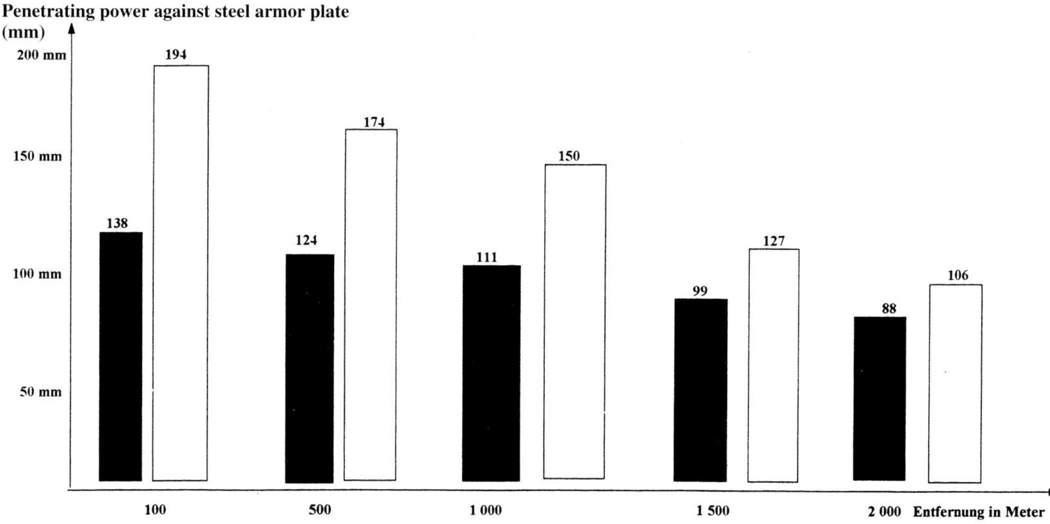

Legend: ■ 7.5 cm Antitank Shell 39/42 □ 7.5 cm Antitank Shell 40/42

Jagdpanzer production raised in its final form to 800 vehicles per month.

The new armament proved to provide considerable improvement in penetrating armor plate. Using the Antitank Shell 39 or 39/42, the values compared to the vehicles with the Tank Destroyer Cannon 39, rose from 81 to 111 mm at 1000 meters. If 7.5 cm Antitank Shells 40/42 were available, even 150 mm of armor gave no protection. The Russian T-34/85 tank could be shot down effortlessly at 1500 meters by both shells; the American "Sherman" even at 2000 meters. The likelihood of hitting a target measuring 2.5 x 2 meters at 1000 meters under combat conditions was 80 to 90 %. Among the Jagdpanzer's other advantages was the low overall height (1.85 meters!), with which, as Guderian wrote in his memoirs, "the limit of the practically bearable in the country" had been reached. The life span of the barrel of this high-performance gun was listed as 2000 to 3000 rounds.

The tank destroyer troops' great need for pursuit tanks resulted in the building of almost unchanged Panzer IV hulls with the 7.5 cm Tank Destroyer Cannon 42 L/70 and solid superstructure. The designation of this variant, createt by the Alkett firm and built at

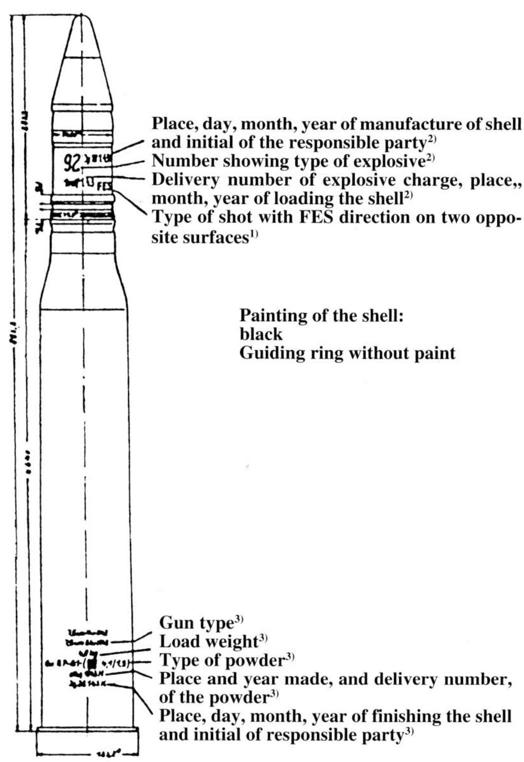

Antitank shell for the 7.5 cm Tank Destroyer Cannon 42.

In August 1944 the Vomag firm of Plauen delivered the first of, in all, 930 Jagdpanzer IV/70(V) (Sd.Kfz. 152/1). With its over-long 7.5 cm Tank Destroyer Cannon 42 and 80 mm front armor, the vehicle was noseheavy and hard to drive off-road..

the Nibelungen Works in Sankt Valentin, was Panzer IV long (A). The fourth solution for a pursuit tank was born in December 1943, first as the idea for a 13-ton heavy assault gun, the Light Tank Destroyer 38(t). The

The Russian counterpart of the Jagdpanzer IV was the SU-85 self-propelled mount, a few examples of which were used by the Army's tank destroyer and assault gun units under the captured-goods designation of SU-85(r). The 85 mm Cannon D-5 S could not penetrate as thick armor as the 7.5 cm Tank Destroyer Cannon 42 chassis, like those of various self-propelled tank destroyer mounts, from the tried and true Czech Panzer 38(t). Armed with the 7.5 cm Tank Destroyer Cannon 39 L/48, the vehicle, weighing barely 16 tons, was notably lighter and more mobile than the Jagdpanzer IV (7.5 cm Pak 39 L/48) (Sd.Kfz. 162). It was used like the Assault Gun III, IV and Pursuit Tank IV in pursuit tank companies with ten or fourteen guns. During the course of 1944, the pursuit tanks developed according to the tank destroyers' requests replaced at least a part of the assault guns and self-propelled tank destroyer mounts in the divisions' tank destroyer units. Their original designation as a new type of assault gun or a light assault gun showed their relationship with the same-named vehicles of the artillery or assault artillery. The significance of the pursuit tank for antitank defense in the last war year is shown by the following list of all the vehicles built:

Designation	**Number made, time made**
Jagdpanzer IV (7.5 cm Pak 39 L/48)(Sd.Kfz. 162), also new type assault gun with 7.5 cm Pak 39 L/48 on Panzer IV chassis	769 January-November 1944
Panzer IV long (V)(Sd.Kfz. 162/1), also Tank Destroyer IV with 7.5 cm Pak 42 L/70	930 August 1944-March 1945
Panzer IV long (A), also Panzer IV with 7.5 cm Pak 42 L/70	278 August 1944-March 1945
Jagdpanzer 38t (7.5 cm Pak 39 L/48 "Hetzer" (Sd.Kfz. 138/2), also Tank Destroyer 38(t)	2584 April 1944-May 1945
Total	**4561**

Not included in this list are Assault Gun III (Sd.Kfz. 142/1) and IV (Sd.Kfz. 167), which had been given to the tank destroyers since the summer of 1943 as temporary equipment. Also omitted were the numerous test models and projects that existed. They had no influence on the development of the tank destroyer troops.

In December 1944 the establishment of another tank destroyer vehicle was begun, its development accompanied by Hitler's particular interest—the Cannon Schützenpanzerwagen (Sd.Kfz. 251/22). The idea was to install the 7.5 cm Tank Destroyer Cannon 40, which had been towed by the Medium Schützenpanzerwagen Hlk 6 p (Sd.Kfz. 251) in the tank destroyer platoons of the heavy companies of the armored grenadier battalions (armored), in the armored vehicle without wheels. These vehicles were used by the aforementioned tank destroyer platoons (three each) and the armored reconnaissance units (six each) of the armored divisions in 1945. On April 1, 1945 a war structure for Tank Destroyer Company (SPW)(f.G.) No. 1142 became valid. In a division into three platoons, it had nine medium Schützenpanzerwagen (7.5 cm Pak L/46)(Sd.Kfz. 251/22). A similar vehicle was the Heavy Armored Scout vCar ARK (Sd.Kfz. 234/4) with 7.5 cm Tank Destroyer Cannon 40. 87 of them reached the troops by March 1945. This was a makeshift solution to improve the action capability of antitank guns formerly on wheeled mounts. Thus there was no change in the basic trend toward fully armored tank destroyers.

As for the tactics of tank destroyer action, they differed from those of tank destroyer cannons on wheeled mounts, whose successful use required an advantageous firing position (edge or ambush position) and a well-conceived firing plan, in

Delivery of the Cannon-SPW Device 922 (7.5 cm Tank Destroyer Cannon 40 on Medium Schützenpanzerwagen Hl k 6 p (Sd.Kfz. 251/22)) began in December 1944.

According to the war structure of April 1, 1945, tank destroyer companies had nine new Sd.Kfz. 251/22. In the mixed armored scout companies, whose War Structure No. 1162 appeared on the same day, three such vehicles were included.

An Sd.Kfz. 251/22 in a junkyard, seen early in 1945. Beside it is an Assault Gun III (Sd.Kfz. 142/1), Type G, late production with support wheels minus rubber pads.

Tank Destroyer Company (SPW), free structure
(as of April 1, 1945)

- **Company Chief**
  - **Group Leader**
    - one medium SPW (Sd.Kfz. 251/3)
    - one halftrack cycle[1] (Sd.Kfz. 2)
  - **1st Platoon**
    - **Platoon Troop**
    - **Gun Platoon** - with three medium SPW (7.5 cm Pak) (Sd.Kfz. 251/22)
  - **2nd Platoon**
    - **Platoon Troop**
    - **Gun Platoon** - with three medium SPW (7.5 cm Pak) (Sd.Kfz. 251/22)
  - **3rd Platoon**
    - **Platoon Troop**
    - **Gun Platoon** - with thee medium SPW (7.5 cm Pak) (Sd.Kfz. 251/22)
  - **Ammunition Squad**

Total Strength
one medium SPW (Sd.Kfz. 251/3)
nine medium SPW (7.5 cm Pak) (Sd.Kfz. 251/22)
three motorcycles, one a halftrack (Sd.Kfz. 2)
four trucks
62 men

[1] Wenn das Kettenkrad nicht lieferbar,dann le.gl. PKW oder Krad mit Seitenwagen

In August 1944, at the same time as the delivery of the Pursuit Tank IV/70 (V)(Sd.Kfz.162/1). the Nibelungenwerk of Sankt Valentin delivered the first Panzer IV/70(A). Using production Panzer IV chassis, 278 tanks armed with the 7.5 cm Tank Destroyer Cannon 42 appeared by March 1945.

Pursuit Tank IV/70(A) are on their way to the front. At the beginning of April 1945 there were 275 Panzer IV with the long 7.5 cm tank destroyer cannon in service, though only 149 were ready for action.

The Pursuit Tank IV/70(A) was 2.35 meters high, half a meter taller than its counterpart from the Vomag works in Plauen.

uniting the firepower, mobility and armor protection of pursuit tanks and assault guns. They were able to "pursue enemy tanks, meaning fight them by attacking. In addition, they could be used like assault guns for direct support of the infantry." Their specific characteristics allowed them to go into battle immediately under almost all conditions. This was especially true when it became necessary to fight tanks that had broken through the German defenses, lessen the impact of their attacks, and gain time for the arrival of strong German reserves. But pursuit tanks also protected their own infantry's attacks from tank counterattacks. The combat of the pursuit tanks was not bound to a definite line, and their low height allowed a much better suitability to terrain forms and vegetation (in comparison with armored vehicles with turrets). This in turn was an important prerequisite for surprise fire, which was to be striven for in any case. Along with the factors of time and surprise, the unifying of available forces at a decisive place in a tank battle took on greater importance. This was the reason why pursuit tanks were to be applied at least in platoon strength (three or four tanks). Characteristic of the positional value that pursuit tanks and assault guns possessed for antitank defense in 1944-45 was the evaluation of an officer on the Wehrmacht command staff: "The only effective antitank defense was done by the assault gun or pursuit tank, while the s.Pak (mot Z) proved more and more insufficient".

Striking and at the same time confusing is the variety of designations for weapons and vehicles of the tank destroyer troops, which were carried over to the individual structures. Changes in written communication, with all their results, were not lacking. There were several attempts to introduce a system here, characterized by several orders from the Inspector-General of the Armored Troops. As an example, here is a command dated January 10, 1945 (Army High Command/Inspector-General of the Armored Troops/ Army General Staff/Org.Unit No. I/200/45 gKdos...): "Effective immediately, the former Tank Destroyer companies (formerly Assault Gun units) of the Tank Destroyer units of the infantry, pursuit and mountain divisions, which are equipped with Jagdpanzer 38, Jagdpanzer IV. Assault Guns III or

A Pursuit Tank IV/70(V)(Sd.Kfz. 162/1), photographed in the spring of 1945. Right in the middle of the vehicle (behind the cannon fairing) stands a 7.5 cm Antitank Shell 39/42.

IV, are to be renamed Jagdpanzer companies, retaining their numbers." In the addendum thereto, examples were cited:

a. If a division includes a tank destroyer company (mot Z), this company is given the designation **1. (mot Z) Panzerjägerabteilung** . . .
b. If a division had a pursuit tank company, this company is given the number of the pursuit tank unit with the **suffix 1000.**
c. If divisions have two pursuit tanks companies, then the 2nd Pursuit Tank Company is given the number of its tank destroyer unit with the **suffix 2000.**

The following tactical symbols were introduced as required:

a. Pursuit tank company with Jagdpanzer 38
b. Purtuit tank company with Assault Gun III
c. Pursuit tank company with Jagdpanzer IV or Assault Gun IV

Two examples:

1st Infantry Division, with staff, one tank destroyer company (mot Z), Jagdpanzer company and Flak company:

Staff/tank destroyer unit 1
1st (mot Z) tank destroyer unit 1
3rd (Flak) tank destroyer unit 1
Jagdpanzer company 1001

12th People's Grenadier Division, with staff, one tank destroyer company (mot Z), one Flak company and two Jagdpanzer companies:

Staff/tank destroyer unit 12
1st (mot Z) tank destroyer unit 12
3rd (Flak) tank destroyer unit 12
Jagdpanzer company 1012 (ex-1012 a)
Jagdpanzer company 2012 (ex-1012 b)

The figures for the specified supplies of pursuit tanks, self-propelled tank destroyer mounts and tank destroyer cannons (mot Z) in the tank destroyer units of the divisions added up to a considerable potential force. The masses of the tank destroyers were united in these bands. At the war's end the reality looked different, as a report on the Wehrmacht's supply of tanks and antitank weapons at the beginning of April 1945 shows. The following totals were on hand:

Zimmerite coating on the side armor of a Jagdpanzer IV.

This photo from Normandy in August 1944 shows a Jagdpanzer IV (Sd.Kfz. 162), Type F, giving grenadiers a ride to the front.

627 Jagdpanzer 38, 445 of them ready for action, 275 Jagdpanzer IV or Panzer IV long, 149 ready for action, 2242 self-propelled tank destroyer mounts or 7.5 cm tank destroyer cannons (mot Z)

These numbers, in view of the masses of Red Army tanks in the east and those of the Allies in the west, as well as those in the Italian theater of war, show that the tank destroyer troops scarcely had a chance to intervent decisively in the war. Typical of the situation was a command given by the Commander of Army Group South, General of the Infantry Otto Wöhler, to the commanders of the armies subordinate to him on January 9, 1945. It was first stated: "On the other hand, the Russians, in most cases, after breaking through their own HKL, pushed forward over the HKF into the depths of the area without noteworthy resistance. This fact shows that the antitank defense of all weapons, particularly the artillery, still is not organized uniformly enough. . . . The lack of heavy Pak gunsrequires in every case that the artillery and the Flak must basically be included in the division's antitank defense plan. . . ." Guns were supposoed to be assigned to such firing and changing positions as made antitank defense possible. This had a decisive importance. "Tank field of fire comes before sight concealment! The depth structure and related defensive front must prevent the batteries at the front edge of the artillery space from being overrun, outflanked or attacked from the rear." Obviously, the Russian example had taught them, for the effectiveness of the Russian antitank defenses in the first sector was noted. It was stated: "In our attacks . . . it was shown that the Russians, even in surprise attacks, built up a number of tank traps in the depths of the battlefield in the shortest time, which could be broken only with heavy losses. . . . Basically, the Russians set up their light and medium artillery so that they became tank-stopping positions."

A Tank Destroyer 38(t) with 7.5 cm Tank Destroyer Cannon 40 (Sd.Kfz. 138). Type H. According to H.Dv. 473/5 b "Training Precepts for the Armored Troops", Volume 5 b "Training on the 7.5 cm Pak-Sf. 38" of December 7, 1943, "a spirit of united attacks, clever command, quick utilization of favorable situations, movement and fire" characterized "the Pak-Sf's manner of fighting."

A 7.5 cm Tank Destroyer Cannon 40 in a tank destroyer unit of the Waffen-SS. An SS armored grenadier division in 1944 was supposed to have 34 7.5 cm tank destroyer cannons of this type.

A self-propelled tank destroyer mount (Sd.Kfz. 139) is seen in the summer of 1944 with Tank Destroyer Replacement and Training Unit 4 in Leipzig-Borna.

Tank Destroyer 38(t)(Sd.Kfz. 138), Type M, are shown during training in 1944.

Tank Destroyer II (Sd.Kfz.132): Several vehicles of this type were created in workshops on the front. The 7.5 cm Tank Destroyer Cannon 40/2 was delivered from Germany on request.

The weak armor of the self-propelled tank destroyer mounts (up to 30 mm) and their high bodies eliminated offensive use of these vehicles against enemy tanks or antitank guns in the manner of assault guns or tanks.

Self-propelled tank destroyer mounts, of the Type M "Marder" are seen in a small German city in the winter of 1944-45.

People's Grenadiers make a counterattack in a village, carried out with support from a pursuit tank company. A few people's grenadier divisions had two such units with Jagdpanzer 38 (Sd.Kfz. 138/2).

For the tank destroyer platoons in the armored grenadier battalions (armored), medium Schützenpanzerwagen Hl k 6p (Sd.Kfz. 251) were issued for use as towing vehicles for 5 and 7.5 cm Tank Destroyer Cannon 38 and 40.

A tank destroyer company with 8.8 cm Rocket Panzerbüchse 54 "Panzer-schreck" is shown in Italy. These were small self-propelled mounts; the Armored Machine-gun carrier Br. 732 (e) served only as transport vehicles for weapons, ammunition and crews.

On the march, the barrel of the 7.5 cm Tank Destroyer Cannon 40 had to be secured to the self-propelled mount to avoid damage to the aiming and targeting apparatus.

In the use of self-propelled tank destroyer mounts, the unified use of the companies was to be striven for as much as possible. Platoon action was allowed. The smallest combat unit was the half-platoon with two tank destroyers. Experience showed that the use of individual vehicles resulted in loss, and thus it was prohibited.

Older self-propelled tank destroyer mounts were used for training in the replacement and training units.

Self-propelled tank destroyer mounts led the firefight from previously located firing positions. The directions called especially for the high performance of this weapon not be misused for premature opening of fire.

Late opening of fire increased the accuracy and penetrating power of the gun and also limited the ammunition consumption.

In the last months of World War II, Assault Gun III (Sd.Kfz. 142/1) and IV (Sd.Kfz. 164) were also found in large numbers in the tank destroyer units.

Because of its low weight and powerful armament, the Jagdpanzer 38 (Sd.Kfz. 138/2) was highly regarded. Early in April 1945 there were 627 vehicles of this type on hand, of which 445 were ready for action.

Two Assault Gun III (Sd.Kfz. 142/1) of Assault Gun Brigade 276 are shown near Kanenez-Podolsk in the spring of 1944. The differentiation of tank destroyer and assault gun units had causes that resulted from the Army's complex organization structure. There task was and remained the same: to destroy tanks.

Between January and November 1944, 769 Jagdpanzer IV (Sd.Kfz. 162), Type F, were delivered. The first vehicles of this type went to the "Hermann Goering" Armored Paratroop Division, the 4th and 5th Armored Divisions, and the Armored Instructional Division.

To cool the barrel of the 7.5 cm Tank Destroyer Cannon 39 after long activity, it was recommended that the barrel be raised as high as possible and all hatches plus the breech be opened (D 1881 "7.5 cm Tank Destroyer Cannon 39 (L/48" of September 1, 1944).

The Jagdpanzer IV (Sd.Kfz. 162), Type F, was about two meters high. The firing height is listed as 1.4 meters. For firing from the tank destroyer cannon, five different types of explosive shells were available (hollow-charge types were included as explosive ammunition).

XI. Army Tank Destroyer Troops in the Last War Year

At the beginning of 1944, the Army had 22 tank destroyer units with 8.8 cm guns; 14 of them had self-propelled mounts of pursuit tanks, the rest had 8.8 cm Tank Destroyer Cannons (mot Z). There was also one independent tank destroyer company, as well as one fast unit. In the Army troops there were nine tank destroyer units, which as a rule had self-propelled tank destroyer mounts (7.5 or 7.62 cm). At this time, several were being rearmed and were supposed to get a mixed supply of self-propelled mounts and 7.5 cm Tank Destroyer Cannons (R.S.O.). Already mentioned elsewhere were the tank destroyer battalions with 8.8 cm Rocket Panzerbüchse 54.

The most important weapon of the Army tank destroyer units was the 8.8 cm gun, which was used on wheeled mounts by eight units. The disadvantages arising from the weapon's great weight have already been noted. Naturally, this applied particularly to the Model 43/41 on a wheeled mount. Even though the more modern version, the 8.8 cm Tank Destroyer Cannon 43 on a cross-axle mount, was better suited for antitank action because of its all-around firing ability, the weight of 3.7 tons in firing position showed all too clearly the limits of this artillery gun's use by the tank destroyers. Its production was raised from 139 in March to 232 in December 1944, but its supply among the troops still stayed within limits; at the beginning of April 1945 there were 531 8.8 cm Tank Destroyer Cannons (mot Z) on hand.

A 12.8 cm gun that was intended as an antitank weapon, like some of the 8.8 cm cannons, saw service with the artillery from the start in its motor-towed version. Because of its high weight, its installation on so-called weapon carriers was considered at the beginning of 1944. The development of these interesting vehicles came to an end for the 8.8 cm gun, and except for a few cases, they were no longer seen among the troops to the end of the war.

The backbone of the other 14 tank destroyer units in 1944 was the "Nashorn" self-propelled tank de-

On April 10, 1945 there were 85 "Nashorn" (Rhinoceros) Tank Destroyer III/IV on hand. Their production had been halted in March 1945.

An 8.8 cm Tank Destroyer Cannon 43/41 (L/71) in firing position. To the right of the gun are three airtight containers for the ammunition of this high-performance gun.

stroyer mount (Sd.Kfz. 164). At the beginning of 1945 there were 141 of them. More and more of these and the few remaining "Elefant" pursuit tanks were being replaced by a new heavy tank destroyer vehicle: the Jagdpanzer V "Jagdpanther" (Sd.Kfz. 173). Its development had been contracted for in the late summer of 1942. In October 1943 the first prototype had been shown at the Arys troop training camp. Between January 1944 and March 1945, 392 pursuit tanks of this type had been delivered. This, probably the best German pursuit tank, was used by Army Tank Destroyer Units 519, 559, 560, 654 and 655, plus a few by tank units. On March 1, 1944 there already appeared, as a preview, War Strength Report No. 1149 a (free) for the heavy tank destroyer company "Panther", according to which each of the three platoons had four pursuit tanks. Two more were with the leader group. With a full supply, the three companies of the tank destroyer unit had considerable firepower. With the 8.8 cm Tank Destroyer Cannon 43/3, the effective shot range increased from 2000 to 3000 meters when sight conditions allowed. At 2000 meters the 8.8 cm Antitank Shell 39/1 could pierce 132 mm of armor plate. This achievement allowed a considerably greater depth effect, at least at focal points of antitank defense, as long as the firepower was combined with effective armor protection and high mobility. The fact that the high hopes for this vehicle were only fulfilled in part was once again caused by its small numbers. At the begining of April 1945 there were only 24 "Jagdpanther" with the troops, although in March 52 had been completed. The small numbers of pursuit tanks compelled several tank destroyer units to be issued a mixed lot of vehicles (for example, Heavy Tank Destroyer Unit 519 had 17 Sd.Kfz. 173 and 28 Sd.Kfz. 142/1) instead of a uniform supply of 45 "Jagdpanther".

Another heavy pursuit tank, the "Jagdtiger", reached the troops as of the autumn of 1944. Between July 1944 and March 1945, 77 of them were delivered. Their use was limited to Heavy Tank Destroyer Units 512 and 653. Technical problems not only delayed delivery but also plagued the action of the 70-ton pursuit tanks. With the 12.8 cm Tank Destroyer Cannon 80 L/55, they could successfully fire on targets at up to 3500 meters. With that, the technical development of the tank destroyer weapon had moved into border areas of weapons and weight that [p. 164] made its use for pursuing tanks questionable. The penetrating power of 155 mm of armor at 3000 meters could be used very rarely anyway, what with the sighting conditions in the central European area.

On January 26, 1945 Tank Pursuit Brigade 104 was formed and, according to a message from the Army General Staff two days later, subordinated to Armored Reconnaissance Unit 115. This was an attempt to create an armored pursuit entity that could operate in its own hinterlands to localize enemy tank forces and destroy them after determining the direction of their thrust. The combining of the pursuit tank with a strong reconnaissance component is significant. Each of its six units had one very mobile reconnaissance company, well equipped with radio equipment in VW Kübelwagen or Schützenpanzerwagen, while the two pursuit tank companies each had 14 Jagdpanzer 38 "Hetzer" (Sd.Kfz. 138/2) to supply the needed firepower.

We must still mention the bicycle-mounted Army tank destroyer units that were formed in April 1945. Information on their strength and armaments is given in the War Strength Report of April 20, 1945 and in a handwritten, undated note about the uniform structure of tank pursuit units. The latter mentions twelve tank pursuit units or groups. Their personnel were recruited from Hungary, Russia and the Caucasus. They were armed with the Rocket Panzerbüchse and Panzerfaust, marking a low point in Army antitank forces.

In connection with the development of the Army's tank destroyer troops, the establishment of fortress Pak forces since July 1944 should also be noted. Their task was antitank defense in fortresses and defense areas. Like the tank destroyer troops, they were subordinate to the Inspector-General of the Armored Troops. In Handbook 77/7, issued on October 10, 1944 by the General of Antitank Defense of All Weapons under the inspector-General of the Armored Troops, fortress Pak companies, of which the forces noted above were composed, were characterized as follows: "The fortress Pak companies, because of their limited personnel and material supplies, have only a limited fighting value. They are not suited for mobile warfare. Their tasks are:

- Destroying penetrating enemy tank spearheads from prepared backline positions,
- Safeguarding the approach and arrival of German reinforcements.

As for the guns, there was a differentiation between medium and heavy antitank cannons (the term "tank destroyer cannon" was not used). The medium guns included the Model 38 5 cm guns, all 5 and 7.5 cm tank guns in pivot mounts, the 7.5 cm Antitank Gun 97/38 and the 7.62 cm Infantry Cannon Howitzer

A crew's souvenir photo with an 8.8 cm Tank Destroyer Cannon 43 (L/71). The extremely long barrel (6280 mm) can be seen clearly.

In 1‘944-45 several test models of light weapons carriers appeared, meant to carry, among others, the capable 8.8 cm Tank Destroyer Cannon 43. The picture above shows a prototype from the Rheinmetall-Borsig GmbH, the one below a vehicle from the Ardelt Works, with a tank chassis, gun (Model 43/3) and gun shield.

The Jagdpanzer V "Jagdpanther" (Sd.Kfz. 173) was delivered from January 1944 on. The Aar Strength Report for Tank Destroyer Units "Panther" came out early in March 1944.

This "Jagdpanther" was lost in action at the Altdamm bridgehead near Stettin. Early in April 1945 no pursuit tanks of this type were found on the eastern front, and only 24 in the west.

According to a production review by the Army General Staff and the Reich Minister for Armament and War Production on April 11, 1945, 52 "Jagdpanther" had been delivered in March and 42 in February 1945.

290(r)-russ.27-. All the long-barreled guns of 7.5m 7.62 and 8.8 cm calibers were classed as heavy antitank guns. Details of structure and equipment were included in the War Budget Fortress-Pak Company War Structure No. 1147 of September 1, 1944.

The 5 and 7.5 cm guns in pivot mounts (and some 3.7 cm) were weapons usually used in tanks, which were produced as part of the Pak-Aktion "fortress" special action in February and March 1945. There were also tank-turret companies with very varying supplies of usually very obsolete turrets from German or foreign tanks. Because of the performance of its 7.5 cm Tank Gun 42 L/70, the 9.5-ton "Panther" East Wall Turret, 259 of which were to be built according to a memo of August 31, 1944, deserves special note. In a listing of March 26, 1945, 2940 tank turrets and cupolas were mentioned as being prepared for the defense of fortresses and defense areas. All these solutions, born of necessity, lacked one important prerequisite for antitank warfare: mobility. The experiences from all past battles had shown that self-propelled and armored antitank weapons, such as pursuit tanks and assault guns above all else, had the best chances for success.

At the beginning of World War II the tank destroyer troops had arisen with the task of dominating the fight against tanks. Their equipment and armament did not enable them, at this early point, to live up to the imposing title of tank destroyers. During the war there was a development that led to the fully armored tank destroyer, the pursuit tank. Another important result with even greater potential for postwar development took shape when the tank destroyers as special troops for fighting tanks were overburdened with fulfilling that task. The decisive role that the tank played on the battlefield made it necessary to introduce a system of antitank defense for all weapons. In the war Germany lacked the power to make up for the omissions of the past.

A further recognition applies to the competition between the destructive effect of shells and the protective effect of armor, which was marked during the war by a special haste in its development. In Germany, for example, it led to much too heavy tank destroyer cannons and vehicles. New technical solutions, somewhat in the spirit of guided antitank rockets, appeared but no longer influenced the action of the tank destroyer troops.

This photo shows the considerable bulk of the 45.5-ton Jagdpanzer V "Jagdpanther" (Sd.Kfz. 173). At 2.72 meters in height, it was too tall for a tank destroyer vehicle. The front armor reached a thickness of 80 mm (fairing 100 mm).

Between July 1944 and March 1945, 77 Jagdpanzer VI "Jagdtiger" (Sd.Kfz.186) were delivered (three in March and 13 in February 1945). The vehicle, armed with the 12.8 cm Tank Destroyer Cannon 44, weighed 70 tons.

Heavy Army Tank Destroyer Unit, Jagdtiger
As of March 1, 1945

Unit Commander

- **Staff Company** with 3 Jagdpanzer VI Jagdtiger (Sd.Kfz. 186), 8 Flakpanzer IV, 3 Flak Sfl (Sd.Kfz. 7/1)
- **1st Company** with 14 Jagdpanzer VI "Jagdtiger" (Sd.Kfz. 186)
- **2nd Company** with 14 Jagdpanzer VI "Jagdtiger" (Sd.Kfz. 186)
- **3rd Company** with 14 Jagdpanzer VI "Jagdtiger" (Sd.Kfz. 186)
- **Supply Company**
- **Repair Shop Company**

Total Strength
45 Jagdpanzer VI "Jagdtiger" (Sd.Kfz. 186)
5 Recovery Tank (Bergepanther) (Sd.Kfz. 179)
4 Flakpanzer IV (3.7 cm)
4 Flakpanzer IV (2 cm quad)
3 2 cm Flak (Sf.) (Sd.Kfz. 7/1)
14 Medium SPW (Sd.Kfz. 251)

Pictures of a burned-out "Jagdtiger" at Mannheimer Strasse and Dreikönigsstrasse in Schwetzingen, photographed on March 30, 1945.

A fragment of a 7.5 cm tank gun on a pivot mount. This weapon belonged to Fortress Pak Unit XXVII (Dresden) at the end of World War II.

The fortress Pak units laso had large numbers of 5 cm Tank Gun L/42 on pivot mounts. With an antitank shell it could pierce 47 mm of armor at 500 meters.

This turret of a Panzer 38(t) belonged to a tank turret company at the fortress of Frankfurt an der Oder. The 3.7 cm Tank Gun 38(t) could pierce 33 mm of armor at 500 meters.

Structure of a Fortress Pak Company
War Strength Report No. 1147 of September 1, 1944

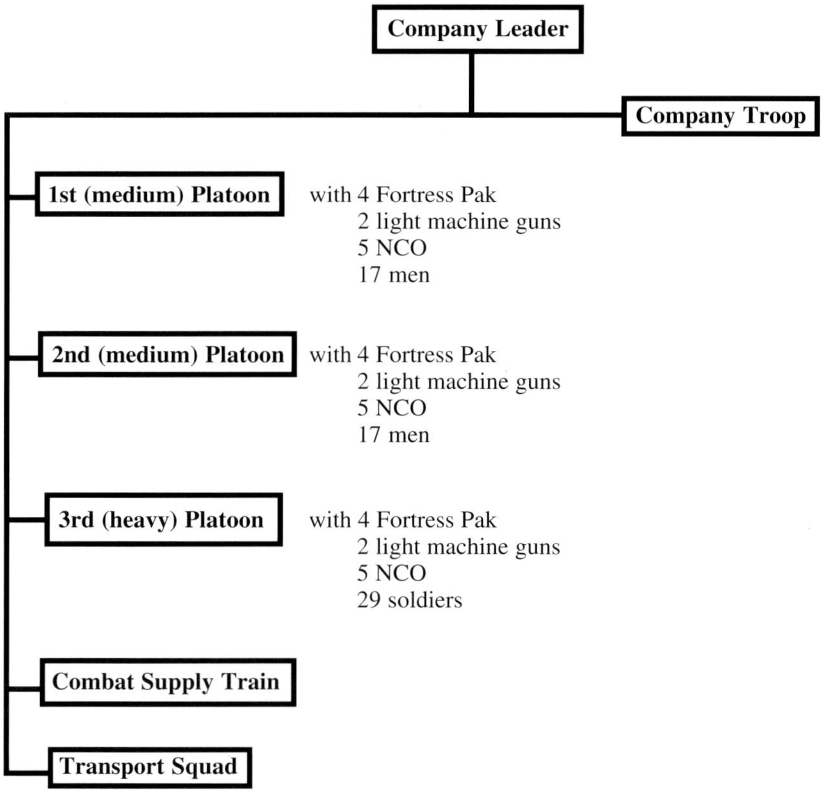

Total Strength
8 medium Fortress Pak
4 heavy Fortress Pak
6 light machine guns

Notes:
1. The gun supply depended on availability. There were differentiations into
a. medium Fortress Pak
-7.62 cm Infantry Cannon Howitzer 290(r)
-7.5 cm Pak 97/38
-7.5 cm Cannon 51 in Pivot Mount I
-7.5 cm Cannon 67 in Pivot Mount I
-5 cm Tank Gun in Pivot Mount I
-7.5 cm Recoilless Cannon
-8.8 cm Rocket Launcher 43
b. heavy Fortress Pak (on wheels or pivot mount)
-7.62 cm Pak 36
-7.62 cm Field Cannon 39(r)
-8.8 cm Pak 43, 43/1, 43/3 or 43/41
-7.5 cm Tank Gun 42 in "Panther" turret

Penetrating Power of German Tank Destroyer Cannons at 500 meter range, at 60-degree angle and armor firmness of 80-100 kg/mm²

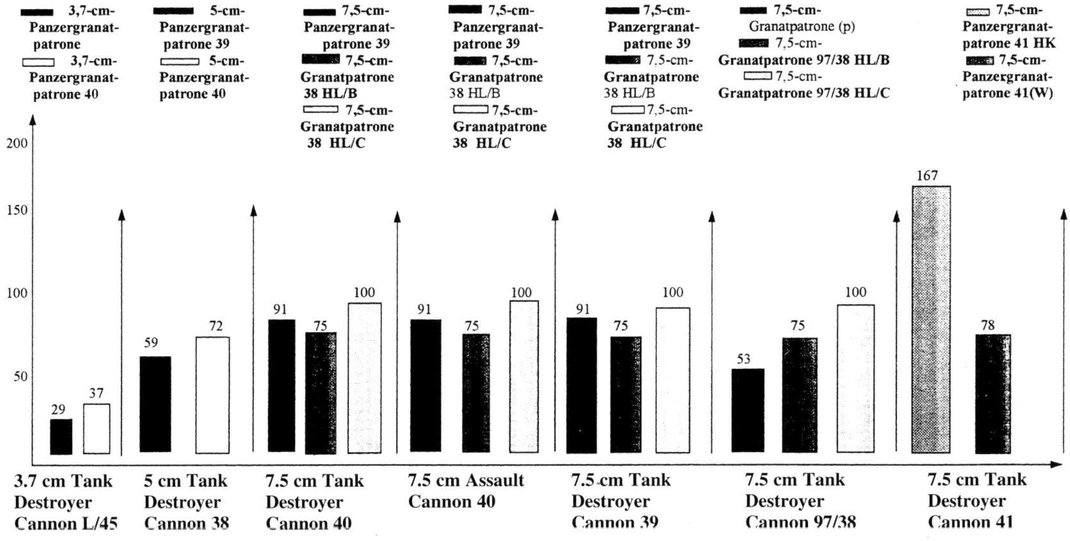

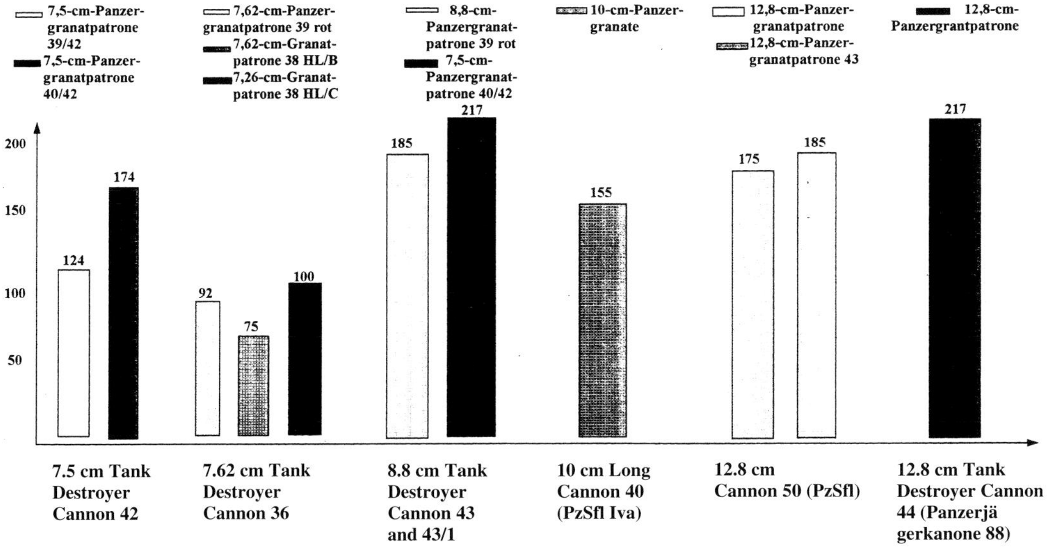

Select Bibliography

H.Dv. 89/4 — The Constant Front, Part 4, The Artillery Battle, 1939

H.Dv. 119/148 — Temporary Shot Table for the 7.62 cm Field Cannon 39 . . ., 1943

H.Dv. 119/312 — Temporary Shot Table for the 5 cm Tank Gun in makeshift pivot mount, 1943

H.Dv. 119/313 — Shot Table for the 5 cm Tank Destroyer Cannon 38, 1943

H.Dv. 119/320 — Shot Table for the 7.5 cm Tank Gun, 7.5 cm Assault Gun, 19040

H.Dv. 119/325 — Temporary Shot Table for the 7.5 cm Tank Gun 422 and 7.5 cm Assault Gun 42, 1943

H.Dv. 119/329 — Temporary Shot Table for the 8.8 cm Tank Gun 43 (L/71), 8.8 cm Tank Destroyer Cannon 43/2 (L/71), 8.8 cm Tank Destroyer Cannon 43/3 (L/71), 8.8 cm Tank Destroyer Cannon 43/41 (L/71), 1944

H.Dv. 130/5 — Training Manual for the Infantry, Volume 5, The Infantry Tank Destroyer Company, various editions, 1938 and 1941

H.Dv. 130/5a — Training Manual for the Infantry. Volume 5a, The Infantry Antitank Company, Individual Training, 1938

H.Dv. 393 — The 3.7 cm Antitank Cannon, 1940

H.Dv. 447/5 — The Tank Gun 14 Kp and Rh., 1927

H.Dv. 469/2-4 — Antitank Defense for All Weapons, verious volumes and editions, 1942-1944

H.Dv. 470/6 — Guide for the Training of Antitank Units, 1935

H.Dv. 470/12 — Training Manual for the Armored Troops, Volume 12, Temporary Guidelines for the Action and Command of the Tank Destroyer Unit. 1941

H.Dv. 470/19 — Firing Guide for Tank, Tank destroyer and Assault Gun Commanders and Aiming Gunners, 1944

H.Dv. 473/1a — Guidelines for the Training of Armored Troops in the Replacement Army: Guidelines for the Training of Troops of a Tank Destroyer Training Unit, 1943

H.Dv. 473/5a	Training Manual for the Armored Troops, Volume 5a, Training on the 7.5 cm Tank Destroyer Cannon 40 (mot Z), 1943
H.Dv. 473/5b	Training Manual for the Armored Troops, Volume 5b, Training on the 7.5 cm Pak-Sf. 38, 1944
H.Dv. 481/177	Handbook for Ammunition of the 4.7 cm Pak 181(f), 1942
H.Dv. 481/42	Handbook for Ammunition of the 7.62 cm Tank Destroyer Cannon 36, 1942
H.Dv. 481/73	Handbook for Ammunition of the 3.7 cm Tank Destroyer Cannon, various editions, 1938 and 1940
H.Dv. 481/30	Handbook for the 3.7 cm Stick Grenade 42(t) for the 3.7 cm Tank Destroyer Cannon 37(t), 1942
H.Dv. 481/501	Handbook for the 3.7 cm Stick Grenade 41 for the 3.7 cm Antitank Cannon, 1943
D 50/5	Handbook of Foreign Equipment, Volume 4: Light Guns, 1941
D 87	Handbook for the Defense of Armored Vehicles, 1932
D 87	Guidelines for Antitank Defense for All Weapons, various editions, 1936 and 1940
D 140	Instructions for Carrying Out Firing Training with the 3.7 cm Antitank Cannon, various editions, 1940 and 1941
D 186	The 5 cm Tank Gun in Makeshift Pivot Mount, 1942
D 228	Instruction Book for Firing on Tanks, 1938
D 638/1a-2	Tracked Tractor East, various editions, 1943 and 1944
D 653/39	Jagdpanzer IV Type F, temporary equipment description, 1944
D 1864/1	Panzerschreck 8.8 cm-RPzB 54, Operating Manual, 1944
D 1864/5	Completion of D 1864/1, 1944
Deutsch, Fr. W.	Theory of Weapons, Berlin, 1939
Guderian, Heinz	Achtung—Panzer!, Stuttgart, no year

Guderian, Heinz	Memoirs of a Soldier, Stuttgart, 1986
Halder, Franz	War Diary, Volume 2, Stuttgart, 1963
Halder, Franz	War Diary, Volume 3, Stuttgart, 1964
Justrow, Karl	The Technical War, Berlin, 1938
Hustrow, Karl	The Technical War, Volume 2, Berlin, 1939
Nehring, Walter	Tank Destruction, Berlin, 1941
Senger und Etterlin, F. M. von	The German Tanks 1926-1945, Munich 1968

German Panzers on the Offensive
Russian Front • North Africa 1941-1942
R.H.S. Stolfi

The German Army conducted offensive military operations more effectively than any other in the twentieth century. Its unparalleled tactical and operational virtuosity is obscured by the politically conditioned circumstance of its defeat in the century's two great wars. Writers on the Second World War compound the obscuration by thin treatment of the early German victories and exaggerated emphasis on the ponderous Allied trek to victory later in the war. The acknowledged superiority of the German Army in battle fighting, however, is exemplified by the offensives of 1939-1942, and German Panzers on the Offensive combines description and interpretation of the advances of nine German panzer divisions to reveal extraordinary details of the great victories. The author has based the study almost entirely on the division war diaries and is able to take the reader aboard the command and combat vehicles, escort him through the fighting, and extract reasons for German success in offensive maneuver war. Based as it is on primary source material, the book presents an authoritative and original interpretation of German success and not the familiar synthesis of secondary sources. The interpretation is constructed in enough detail to be a realistic basis for improvement of present-day military operations by the professional and to fascinate and inform the general reader.

Size: 6" x 9" Illustrations: over 50 b/w photos, maps Pages: 224
ISBN: 0764317709 hard cover $35.00